Lightness and Soul
Musings on Eight Jewish Writers

Lightness and Soul
Musings on Eight Jewish Writers

By J.S. Porter

Seraphim
EDITIONS

Copyright © 2011 J.S. Porter

All rights reserved. No part of this publication may be reproduced or transmitted in any form or by any means – electronic or mechanical, including photocopying, recording or any information storage and retrieval system – without written permission from the publisher, except by a reviewer who wishes to quote brief passages for inclusion in a review.

The publisher gratefully acknowledges the financial assistance of the Canada Council for the Arts.

Canada Council for the Arts   Conseil des Arts du Canada

Library and Archives Canada Cataloguing in Publication

Porter, J. S., 1950-
  Lightness and soul : musings on eight Jewish writers / J.S. Porter.

ISBN 978-1-927079-02-7

  1. Jewish literature–20th century–History and criticism.
2. Jews–Intellectual life–20th century. 3. Jewish authors–Biography.
I. Title.

PN842.P67 2011   809'.88924   C2011-905313-6

Editor: George Down
Author Photo: Frances Ward
Cover Design and Typography: Julie McNeill, McNeill Design Arts

Published in 2011 by
Seraphim Editions
54 Bay Street
Woodstock, ON
Canada N4S 3K9

Printed and bound in Canada

Wake up ... And pay attention to the world.

Susan Sontag

For my family

*Cheryl; Daniel, Wanh & Kaizen;
Rachel, Chris, Brayden & Kalen;
Caroline & Andy; Karen & Jim;
Lil; Anna & John*

Contents

Author's Note		11
I	I, Reader and The People of the Book(s)	15
II	Alberto Manguel at Read	27
III	Robert Lax: Syllable and Word	39
IV	Notes on John Berger and Simone Weil	56
V	Muriel Rukeyser: In Each Word a Storm	70
VI	Leonard Cohen and the Power of the Strange	83
VII	Harold Bloom's Jesus	96
VIII	The Last Jewish Intellectuals: Susan Sontag and Edward Said (or, Two New Yorkers Reading and Writing)	111
Closing Time		126
Memorable Quotes		133
Where do books come from?		140
Acknowledgements		141

Author's Note

For a time I jokingly thought of calling this book "2 Gentiles & 7½ Jews". The ½ Jew is Simone Weil, someone who was reluctant to acknowledge her Jewishness. The Nazi administration in occupied France didn't share her reticence. The gentiles are Edward Said, who once towards the end of his life – not altogether spoofingly – referred to himself as "the last Jewish intellectual", and me.

Each chapter in the book has to do with an encounter I've had with a specific Jewish writer. The Czech novelist Milan Kundera defines an encounter as "a spark; a lightning flash; random chance". My encounters sometimes entail sparks, flashes and chance, and sometimes don't.

My first encounter with Harold Bloom took place because of my reading his editing and annotating works by William Blake. Robert Lax seeped into my reading life through the work of his friend Thomas Merton. John Berger came by spark and flash; Muriel Rukeyser, more by chance. My acquaintance with Alberto Manguel came about through assignments from the *Globe and Mail* and the *Literary Review of Canada*. Susan Sontag, with her raven-black hair and alluring shock of white, seduced me by a photograph, or maybe I first read her essay on the eroticism of reading and her words seduced me. Edward Said, I can't remember, maybe in a literature class; Simone Weil I encountered through the Canadian philosopher George Grant. As for Leonard Cohen, you can't live awake in Canada without having a nodding acquaintance with him as a singer or a poet.

Some of my selected writers speak to each other, which makes them more than a heterogeneous group conveniently Christo-wrapped under the banner of "Jewish authors". Said has things to say about Sontag, Berger and Bloom, Sontag has things to say about Berger, and both Berger and Sontag have things to say about Weil. Simone Weil was also an important part of Robert Lax's reading and is quoted by Alberto Manguel in his book on Homer. No one reads or writes in complete isolation. There is usually someone holding your hand or standing over your shoulder as you turn pages.

Literary critic Alfred Kazin once asked himself facetiously who he would read if he couldn't read anti-Semites. In similar vein, I interrogate myself: who would I read if not Jews? My idea of a novelist is Philip Roth; a poet, Mark Strand; a critic, Susan Sontag. Many of the deepest reads of my life have been my encounters of Jewish writers and thinkers, going back to Isaac Singer's novels and Saul Bellow's translation from the Yiddish of his long short story "Gimpel the Fool". In the pages that follow I trace the literary steps of a slate of Jewish luminaries.

My one gentile scholar is the Palestinian-American Edward Said, who, in the final years of his life, was exploring Jewish thinkers, Freud among them, with attention and appreciation. You simply can't love language and books without encountering Jews along the way.

My Jewish writers follow a particular path in an old Jewish tradition: commitment to study and debate, reverence for the book and respect for the word. My Jews are for the most part secular with no particular concern for Judaism (Leonard Cohen and Muriel Rukeyser are exceptions) and no particular attachment to the State of Israel. Historian Isaac Deutscher would be inclined to call them "non-Jewish Jews", but that oxymoron implies a hierarchy of Jewishness – that some Jews are more Jewish than others.

My authors range from the apolitical Robert Lax to the very political John Berger; they exhibit gradations of pride in their Jewish heritage and varying degrees of interaction with their tradition. John Berger has been mostly silent on his heritage; Robert Lax was also a Catholic; Leonard Cohen from time to time has incorporated Zen Buddhism and Catholicism into the rhythm of his life and writings, although as recently as November 2007 in *Border Crossings* he can declaim proudly, "… I'm a practicing Jew, and I always was …" Alberto Manguel doesn't say much about his Jewish heritage in his books, although in his columns for the Vancouver magazine *Geist* – mostly recently in the Summer 2008 issue – he speaks movingly of his familial heritage. Susan Sontag didn't say a great deal about being a Jew. In many ways, one is inclined to regard her as a New Yorker first.

There are many strands in anyone's fabric of identity and each individual chooses to emphasize or de-emphasize certain of the strands. One's Jewishness can be played up or played down or, in the case of Simone Weil, not played at all. "To be a Jew in the twentieth century/Is to be offered a gift …" Muriel Rukeyser reminds her readers. Weil refused the gift. She also refused the gift of Catholicism although she thought within its framework. The Nazis defined her as a Jew, and she went into exile on the basis of her Jewishness, and yet she never accepted Jewishness as a part of her identity. In her mind, her intellectual inheritance was French and Greek. Is one still a Jew if one decides not to be?

Muriel Rukeyser wasn't shy about her Jewishness, and Harold Bloom isn't shy about his, even though his way of being Jewish seems primarily to consist of reading a great many books and commenting on as many as possible. Can one be exclusively a literary Jew? Yes, if polyglot George Steiner is right in asserting, "Addiction to textuality has characterized, continues to characterize Jewish practice and sentiment." Further: "No other community in the evolution and social history of man, has from its outset, read, reread without cease, learnt by heart or by rote, and expounded without end the texts which spell out its whole destiny."

As a solitary reader, I'm drawn to a tradition that encourages questions and debate, self-examination and self-challenge, a tradition that doesn't separate the word from the book or the book from the spirit. Spiritbookwords are an important part of my individual consciousness; they also form a part of the consciousness of the individuals I write about.

My selected writers take seriously what they perceive as "a moral obligation to be intelligent", to be alert and awake and engaged. They also have a spiritual dimension, which in some cases may simply mean that they have poetic and imaginative dimensions beyond what happens to flesh or can be accounted for by flesh. Magic, as Leonard Cohen memorably says in his novel *Beautiful Losers,* is always afoot.

I, Reader and The People of the Book(s)

I read. I dream. I take notes. I write.

Reading is what I do. Reader is who I am. I write books on my readings, books on other people's books, and construct sentences from other people's sentences. My words sometimes turn up as anonymous fragments on the covers of other people's books. If I could only declare one item of identification at the border, it would be reader.

I like books in the same ways I like dogs. I like the look of them, the feel of them, the smell of them. My heart quickens when I see someone reading. I feel most myself when turning and underlining pages.

I like to look at pictures of people reading. I enjoy Vermeer's painting of a woman reading, and Van Gogh's, and Edward Hopper's many paintings of women reading. A particularly striking painting is by Gustav Adolph Hennig of a young dark-haired woman reading a small dark-covered book. The painting is called *Girl Reading,* 1828. It was used as the cover for the German edition of Alberto Manguel's *A History of Reading.* The girl has a look of concentration, even reverence, towards what she holds in her hands.

The most telling portrait of me is the picture my wife took of me in New Mexico. I'm lying on a bed covered from head to toe in books. My favourite photograph of my father is the one taken of him lying on a Mexican beach with a book and a pen in his hand. The supine position seems ideal for reading. I like to look at pictures of family members reading. One of my favourites is a photograph of my son reading to my grandson. The picture was taken when my grandson was 3½ months old. On his wedding day, my son gave me a picture of me reading to him when he was about 2½ years old.

My father read poetry, theology, biography and philosophy in that descending order of significance. The book was his means of transportation, his airplane to elsewhere, his frigate out of Ireland. He took to heart Wordsworth's words: "Dreams, books, are each a world." In descending order of significance, I read poetry, life stories (in which I include biography, autobiography, memoir, diaries, journals and letters), theology, art and literary criticism, and books of ideas. For both Dad and me, the book, in Ezra Pound's memorable phrasing, was "a ball of light" in our hands. It stored our dreams, exercised our imaginations and developed our hearts.

Professor Daniel Coleman, in his *In Bed with the Word*, writes: "Reading is not solely an exercise to feed one's inner life. Rather, eating the book – not just nibbling at it, or having a little taste here and there, but eating it wholesale – produces a changed person, an empowered person, a different kind of person …" Dad shared Daniel's hunger, and so do I.

Words were always potentially revolutionary for my father – life-altering, especially words in a book. He always gave me the impression that he believed that a great book could turn him around, reposition him in the world, remake him in some fundamental way, in much the same way as Proust was remade by his reading and translating John Ruskin and that Gandhi was remade by reading a single work by Ruskin.

Recently I've come across V.S. Naipaul talking about a book Gandhi read on the train from Johannesburg to Durban in South Africa. The book was John Ruskin's *Unto this Last* and by the time Gandhi arrived in Durban, a twenty-four-hour journey, he was transformed. Ruskin, Gandhi said, brought out "the latent goodness in his own heart".

Gandhi learned three things from Ruskin's book. First, the good of the individual is in the good of the all; secondly, a barber's work is as important as a lawyer's; and thirdly, the life of labour, physical labour involving the hands, by craftsmen or tillers, is a life worth living. It may not be an exaggeration to say that Gandhi formulated the germ of the Indian Revolution by his encounter with a book on a train. Weaving and cottage industries – works of the hands – became his defiant way of resisting the commercial power of an empire.

Reading the letters of St. Paul and the parables of Jesus had an electrifying influence on my father. The letters and stories contained in an ancient book sowed the seeds of his own personal revolution, the remaking of his self. He was to supplement his remaking by the poets, particularly Shakespeare and Wordsworth, but no subsequent exposure to books had the transformative power of his early encounters with the New Testament. It brought out "the latent goodness in his own heart".

What, if anything, has brought out the latent goodness of my heart? Works by Robert Lax and Simone Weil and John Berger have, to some extent. Berger's refusal to abandon ethics at the altar of aesthetics (Bloom would be unforgiving of such misplaced high-mindedness), Weil's refusal of the easy life, the easy way, Lax's and Cohen's insistence on play as a form of sacrament. These writers, along with a strange monk from Kentucky, and a handful of others, have opened my mind and kept my heart from closing.

You read alone. You write alone. Most of the time. Not always. Jacob Lawrence's painting *The Library* with its multitude of readers turning pages, used as the front cover of Nadine Gordimer's *Writing and Being,* suggests that we sometimes read in company. A public library is a public reading space. In certain ways, you write alone and in company. You write alongside elders and ancestors and sometimes, if Harold Bloom is right in his theory, against them. You read for the dead as well as the living.

My selected authors in this book are readers as well as writers. Susan Sontag says it well: "A writer is first of all a reader. It is from reading that I derive the standards by which I measure my own work and according to which I fall lamentably short." What one reads sits in judgment of what one writes; reading is the standard by which the quality and worth of writing is measured.

Sontag goes on: "It is from reading, even before writing, that I became part of a community – the community of literature – which includes more dead than living writers." Sontag has the order right: first one reads, then one writes. She also has the ratio of the dead relative to the living in the right proportion. Of my authors only Bloom, Berger, Cohen and Manguel are still living. All, the living and the dead, belong to the community of readers and writers.

A particular one-word cluster stands out for me in Edmond Jabès' *The Book of Questions.* "I is a book." One of the things the sentence means, it seems to me, is: the "I" is built by books; the self comes into being from seeing its reflection in the mirror of books. Once upon a time that was so. The self is built by other things now, by three screens in particular: television, movie and computer. I is a screen. Throw in video games and music and you have several important building blocks of contemporary selfhood. But this self, this I, the I that is speaking to you, was built by books. My father was also built by books.

The book is a slow technology. Reading requires an investment of time, patience and concentration. It also insists on stillness and slowness. You don't motor through Shakespeare the way you would motor through a rerun of Seinfeld, fast-forwarding as you go. You can't read Henry James in a hurry.

Speed seizes our lives now and it doesn't graciously tolerate indulgences in the slow turning of pages or in the slow dreaming that accompanies the turning. I had time for dreaming in my childhood, time for the slow turning of pages. Dad, being a full-time worker at 14, had less time for dreaming, but he somehow got exposed to a book he cherished all his adult life – *Palgrave's Golden Treasury,* a book designed for dreaming.

Dad cloaked me in poetry by making available to me a fairly extensive library in poetry, but more importantly through records on a turntable. His playing, and my listening to, English actors reading from Blake, Wordsworth, Keats and Shakespeare had an enormous impact on my ear. His taking me to Stratford in my preteens to see Shakespeare's cycle of history plays also provided recurring music in my ear, a seashell with the sea's roar.

I don't know the biography of John Berger well enough to know if he was similarly blessed by his father, but lines from one of his poems ring true to my experience:

> My heart born naked
> was swaddled in lullabies.

> Later alone it wore
> poems for clothes.
> Like a shirt
> I carried on my back
> the poetry I had read.

I carry on my back the poetry I've read, the poetry I've listened to.

Dad also made sure that we had good journals and newspapers coming into the house. We had subscriptions to *The Saturday Review* edited by Norman Cousins, *The Guardian Weekly* which, at the time, contained full supplements from *Le Monde* and *The Washington Post,* and a Scottish theological journal called *The Expository Times.* He also made sure I was familiar with the English journals *Encounter* and *The New Statesman.*

"Live as though all your ancestors were living again through you." These are the words from the ancient Greeks that the poet Ted Hughes shared with his son. My variation on the theme is: Read as though the dead were still living in you. I read for my dead father and my dead friend Mark Garber, as a pregnant woman eats for two, for her own nourishment and the nourishment of the life within her. I read for the living spirits within me. My reading of books on Shakespeare, for instance, is a way of carrying on my father's reading in literary criticism.

Friend and fellow writer Marilyn Gear Pilling says that I read piggishly, with full body engagement. My tongue and teeth sink into a book, my skin tingles, my spine shivers.

Divide the world

> into those who tiptoe into
> the hallowed chapel
> of the book, wearing gloves
> and those who roll
> in the written word
> as a pig rolls
> in the slob slop
> of the unmucked pen ...

She numbers me as one of the ones rolling in the slob slop, in the unmucked pen. I tell her that I'm happy to be among the pigs. I always thought that Orwell gave pigs a bum rap in *Animal Farm* by making them the tyrants.

My wife recently bought me Mahmoud Darwish's *Mural* translated by Rema Hammami and John Berger. She inscribed, "It's a small book you can easily put in your pocket." Berger wrote the introduction and provided drawings with handwritten lines from Darwish's poems. The lines and fragments from Darwish include these:

> *In each thing I see my soul and what I cannot feel hurts me.*
> *And what doesn't feel the hurt my soul causes, it also hurts me.*
> *... the land of my poem is green ...*
> *And the welcome is as warm as bread.*
> *How am I born from a thing I later make?*

These lines and others like them share the page with Berger's lines of a human face or a flower.

As Berger was mourning the death of Palestine's national poet on August 9th, 2008, his hand began drawing in remembrance of an articulated life. Lines from Darwish's poems began, "like rhizome plants, to intermingle and entwine with the drawn lines" and what resulted was a kind of hybrid of word and image. This book is precious to me because my wife has her hand in it, a poet I admire is present in it, and a poet-critic with immense gifts of the heart and mind is at work in it.

Berger was a gift from Wayne Allan to me. Very early on in our friendship, he would talk about a certain English art critic. The college where we taught owned the BBC tapes, *Ways of Seeing,* and I used them in the classroom whenever I could. I also read Berger's novel, *A Painter of Our Time,* first, on Wayne's recommendation, and then everything I could get my hands on, from *Permanent Red* to *Hold Everything Dear.* Berger, along with Wayne himself, educated my sight.

I count Berger among my heroes, someone who maintains a lively banter in my mind with George Orwell, Albert Camus and Edward Said. They are four artists of the word who committed their lives to defending underdogs.

Several of Berger's lines have entered my consciousness for good, so I pull them out for rethinking, and religious repetition: "The number of lives that enter any one life is incalculable." Berger has always tried to acknowledge the lives that entered his, the lives with whom he has become intimate. He has also written an exquisite line on the writer's duty that I want to take to heart in my own work: "All you have to know is whether you're lying or whether you're trying to tell the truth …"

He's a beautiful mixture of clashing and clanging things: Marxist, Christian, a Jew, an intellectual Englishman who also works with his hands alongside French peasants, a man of words who draws and paints, a walker who also rides a motorcycle, a smoker, a blindingly fast talker and a ploddingly slow writer where every other word is an invitation to pause and reflect.

I have in my hands a black and white photograph by Clemens Kalischer. I wonder if Berger has seen it. I cut the photograph out of the magazine *The Sun*. Sun is about the best word in the language, in any language. *Le soleil* in French, *el sol* in Spanish. The word works beautifully in compounds and hyphenated words: Sun-up, sundown, sunburn, sun-showers, sun-speckled, sun-streaked, sunspots, Sunday and so on.

In the photograph, a man, perhaps 60ish, looks out to the viewer, peering dreamily at the camera or into space in a self-reflective moment. The man sits on a bench near an open window; he is holding an open book in his hands. He is wearing a kippah as worn by observant Jews. His elbow rests on the windowsill, books are stacked to his right, he is comfortably slouching, his right foot under a chair or another bench. Above him is writing in Hebrew, light crosses his face, a fedora lies beside him on the bench. Has he taken off one hat and put on another? His shirt is light-coloured, his pants, skullcap and book cover are dark. He's bearded.

A Jew reading. A Jew at read. In the house of reading, there is always in my imagination at least one Jew reading. Is this anonymous man reading what I read: poetry, politics, theology, biography, autobiography, philosophy? I read with a pen in hand. Does he? Words tap on my ear. I read with my body as well as my mind. Does he?

Bloom likes to say that systematic reading begins with St. Augustine. I don't believe him. For me, reading begins with a Jew. A Jew, probably an anonymous one, not the philosopher-theologian from northern Africa, is the archetypal reader. He's the man in the photograph sitting by a window holding a book.

Sometimes I think of three Jews reading. I think of George Steiner, Harold Bloom and Susan Sontag, three of the great readers of our time. I can see each one as a replacement for the anonymous Jew, sitting on the bench, looking out into space reflectively. I can even visualize each one reading beside the others even though none has had a good word to say about the other two. Wouldn't that be a photograph – the three of them reading together? I shook Steiner's hand. Once. I shook Sontag's hand. Once. I've never had the opportunity to shake Bloom's hand. Any one of them could be in the picture. But they're not. Instead, a single man, a man alone and anonymous, reads.

We readers, aglow in the word, huddle together like penguins against the world's chill, its indifference and amnesia. We're reading all the time, reading the world, reading friends and people we've barely met, reading intentions and motives and emotions, reading books. When you read, you read against the grain of death. You read stubbornly, defiantly. You read desperately, as if looking for a missing child. You read deliriously, in the hope of ecstasy and the fear of the inevitable misreading.

Steiner says that the Jewish homeland is the book. Not Israel, not a chunk of geography or a spot in time, but the transportable book, bound neither by place nor time. It doesn't matter where you are when you read, or at least it doesn't matter very much. You can be in prison, you can be on a boat, you can be near a window. The book is what matters. In a certain sense, the book is more important than you, more important than your culture, country or language. That's what Kalischer tells me in his photograph. He might have chosen a celebrity for his subject. He didn't. He chose an anonymous man with a beard and a skullcap, reading.

As the myjewishlearning.com website notes, while Jews are frequently referred to as "the People of the Book", they "have always been a people of many books ..." Books in Jewish traditions have been a means to enfleshing a phrase associated with Lionel Trilling, "the moral obligation to be intelligent". In addition, they "have become the territory through which and in which Jews have traveled and interacted with other Jews".

Steiner reinforces this thought in *My Unwritten Books:*

The tablet, the scroll, the manuscript and the printed page become the homeland, the moveable feast of Judaism. Driven out of its native ground of orality, out of the sanctuary of direct address, the Jew has made of the written word his passport across centuries of displacement and exile.

Putting experiences into books has helped to ensure the survival of the Jewish people. Steiner, a man of religious temperament and sensibility, although not a man of religious conviction, regards the survival of his battered and buffeted people as a miracle. For some experiences, only the religious vocabulary suffices.

In my imagination, and in Steiner's, there is something deeply Jewish about turning pages, commenting on commentaries, making footnotes, scribbling notes in margins. Steiner solemnly catalogues "the textual proclivities", the ongoing secular Midrash, of Jews and their contributions to "the climate of Western consciousness". Of the principal shapers of that consciousness – Darwin, Freud, Marx and Einstein – only Darwin is a non-Jew.

I would seat a fifth person at the table: Nietzsche, the son of a Lutheran pastor. Nietzsche is a great spawner of isms: existentialism, perspectivism, even deconstructionism. I also do not forget that Jesus of Nazareth and Paul of Tarsus are Jews with worldwide impact.

Jews, in Steiner's imagination, and in mine, are a book-built people. In his chapter called "Zion" from his book on his unwritten books, Steiner asks the question: *Why has the self-designation and designation from without of certain communities and individuals as Jews, however contentious it is, endured?* His answer is the book. If my personal "I" can be book-built, why can't a whole people, allowing for individual exceptions, be book-built? Certainly the forthcoming Jewish writers and readers, the subjects of the following chapters, are book-built.

II Alberto Manguel at Read

ON THE BACK COVER OF Alberto Manguel's *The Library at Night* is a blurb from George Steiner with these words: "A love letter written to reading." And then below Steiner's blurb is one from *The Globe and Mail* with these words: "Alberto Manguel [is] a keeper of the word and a guardian of the book" by an anonymous writer. I am that anonymous writer and the book I was writing about was an early collection of essays entitled *Into the Looking-Glass Wood*. In any case, much of Manguel's work is a love letter to reading and he really is a keeper of the word and a guardian of the book.

Born in Argentina, raised in Israel while his father was the Argentinian ambassador, groomed in Canada where he began to write and publish, Manguel presently resides in France. He's a translator and an anthologist; he's a reader and writer. He's also a book-built man with a story-stocked mind. You can readily picture him at Clemens Kalischer's window reading with the ever-present Jorge Luis Borges at hand.

If Manguel were stopped at one of the many borders he crosses and forced to declare only one nationality, I suspect that, like me, he'd respond, "Reader." It seems to me that, like his mentor Jorge Luis Borges, he is principally a reader. He writes about books and his reading. Consider *A History of Reading* or *With Borges; A Reading Diary* or his book on Homer; his Massey Lectures entitled *The City of Words* or his account of libraries and his own personal library in *The Library at Night*, as well as the patchwork of *A Reader on Reading*. For some years now, Manguel has been constructing a series of meditations on reading – the aesthetics, the eroticism, the ethics of reading.

He reads for consolation. He doesn't elaborate on what he means by consolation. Certainly reading offers its practitioners a measure of consolation. The self, no matter how grand, is small, and life, no matter how dream-extended, is short. Each of us is confined to one life in one time. Each of us by book-vessel can appropriate, kidnap and intersect other selves.

Manguel can't remember a time when he wasn't surrounded by his library. At age seven or eight, he assembled in his room "a minuscule Alexandria, about one hundred volumes of different formats on all sorts of subjects". In his Toronto home, he placed books in bedrooms, the kitchen, corridors and the bathroom. His children complained that they needed a library card to enter their own house. He reads promiscuously. In his dreams he conjures an anonymous library "in which books have no title and boast no author, forming a continuous narrative stream in which all genres, all styles, all stories converge … a stream into which I can dip at any point of its course".

According to the poet-thinker Ralph Waldo Emerson, creative readers are as necessary as creative writers for books to come to life. One of the remarkable aspects of recent books by Alberto Manguel is their implicit invitation to readers to add to them. He invites readers to write as well as read. When he constructs his book of favourite readings in *A Reading Diary: A Passionate Reader's Reflections on a Year of Books,* for example, readers find themselves mentally co-constructing their own lists. He has H.G. Wells' *The Island of Dr. Moreau,* I have Jonathan Swift's *A Tale of a Tub;* he has Goethe's *Elective Affinities,* I have André Breton's *Nadja.*

In *The Library at Night,* Manguel presents, by word and image, some of the significant libraries in the world and of his life, including the "amicable Toronto Reference Library". He spends time with his own personal library in France, The Library at Le Presbytère, which curiously resembles a room in the Library of the Colegio Nacional de Buenos Aires. Manguel lives with about 30,000 books. He likes to read in, or just peer at, the library at night "when the library lamps are lit, the outside world disappears and nothing but this space of books remains in existence".

He surveys the library through a suite of metaphoric lenses: the library as Order, Power, Chance, Mind, Imagination, Identity and Home, among others. He reflects on the burnt library of Alexandria, the personal libraries of Montaigne, Rabelais, Borges and Adolph Hitler, biblioburros in Colombia – the rough equivalent of our bookmobiles – and the spectacularly bequeathed library of Aby Warburg in his chapter "The Library as Mind". Here Manguel is at his storytelling best.

Warburg, the son of a Jewish banker, can't reconcile himself to his father's banking empire or religious orthodoxy, and so retreats into books. On his 13th birthday, Aby Warburg offers his younger brother Max his birthright. He turns the family firm over to Max in exchange for a pledge that Max will buy him all the books he desires. These Max-purchased books – my kingdom for a book! – become the core of his library. As Warburg imagines it, a library is above all an accumulation of associations, each association breeding a new image or text of potential connectedness, until the associations return the reader to the first page. For Warburg, every library is circular. Incorporated into the University of London in the 1940's, The Warburg Institute houses over 350,000 volumes.

As Manguel conducts his tour of some of the world's grand libraries, I find myself dreaming of Hemingway's cat-cluttered tropical library outside Havana, a vine-enwrapped house I've only seen in pictures. The white-bearded Papa stands on a ladder and reaches for the top shelf. I picture myself at the Trinity College Library looking at the *Book of Kells* and the marble busts of the Irish greats, Swift among them. I imagine the library as a snake-pit: one good bite and you go away altered. I see the history of libraries as the history of the world's choirs: the best songs sung by the best voices.

Libraries are hives of honey where the readers' tongues lick off the sweetness, cemeteries where lips kiss the dead into life, houses of memory where amnesia is not allowed to enter, sanctuaries of light against the threatening dark. Libraries are where books go to be preserved. But are the books read into life or are they merely stored specimens in formaldehyde? Are libraries Andy Goldsworthy sculptures built to perish or Michelangelo marbles made to last? Immortality may not be possible for the individual or even the species, but what about the species' thoughts and dreams?

The World Wide Web, a virtual library, conceivably traps and preserves every human document which crosses its path. It's the most comprehensive storage system ever devised. In theory, everyone with a portable computer and the Internet has access to thousands, if not millions, of books. And yet this virtual library seems as vulnerable as a physical library, just as fragile, susceptible to deletion or human and electronic failure.

Manguel's response to web libraries is critical. "The Web, and its promise of a voice and a site for all," he says, "is our equivalent of the *mare incognitum,* the unknown sea that lured ancient travelers with the temptation of discovery." The Web promises eternity but it delivers ephemera. Seventy per cent of its communications, posits Manguel, lasts less than four months.

Comparing the Library of Alexandria to the World Wide Web, Manguel writes, "One aspired to include everything, the other will include anything, without context, a constant present, which for Medieval scholars was a definition of hell." All things webbed and Googled stress velocity over reflection and brevity over complexity. A Borgesian dream of completeness shape-shifts into a nightmare of drivel. If there is no discriminating hand of editors, publishers and librarians, the library of everything descends into the library of nothing. As Manguel puts it, "On the Web, where all texts are equal and alike in form, they become nothing but phantom text and photographic image."

In any case, the dream of a complete library, either electronically or in book form, is unrealizable. Already too much is lost and irretrievable. As Manguel reminds us, "Of Aeschylus' 90 plays only 7 have reached us; of the 80-odd dramas of Euripides, only 18; of the 120 plays of Sophocles, a mere 7." How many more Gospels remain in Egyptian caves? Where is the complete Sappho? As philosopher Jacques Derrida says in "Plato's Pharmacy", "[P]erpetually and essentially, texts run the risk of becoming definitively lost. Who will ever know of such disappearance?"

Think of the ransacked and looted Iraqi National Archives, the Archaeological Museum and the National Library of Baghdad. "Much of the earliest recorded history of humankind was lost to oblivion," claims Manguel, underlining once again the vulnerability and fragility of libraries. Throughout history, they have been at the mercy of flood, fire, earthquake and war.

Even without such dramatic intervention, the book's fate, like the human being's, is to die. Like flesh itself, the book – even when preserved in libraries – ages, decays and eventually decomposes. Such synchronicity with the human life cycle may be another reason why many readers, Manguel included, prefer the book to the chip.

One of the surprise entries in Alberto Manguel's book of libraries is his cataloguing of Adolf Hitler's personal library. Who would suspect such a broad range of books from such a narrow-minded man? "In the spring of 1945, a group of American soldiers of the 101st Airborne Division discovered, hidden in a salt mine near Berchtesgaden, the remains of the library of Adolf Hitler, 'haphazardly stashed in schnapps crates with the Reich Chancellery address on them'."

Hitler's original library, estimated at 16,000 volumes, ranged from military history to the arts, spirituality and popular fiction. He collected a handful of classic novels: *Gulliver's Travels, Robinson Crusoe, Uncle Tom's Cabin* and *Don Quixote*. How can one read *Don Quixote* and not confront one's own delusions? Why didn't *Gulliver's Travels,* one of the great anti-war tracts in literature, teach Hitler something about human vanity and the human capacity, on occasion, for understanding and kindness?

Having a library is of course no guarantee that one actually reads the books or understands them. Is it possible to read primarily to buttress one's own prejudices and predilections? Like Manguel, Timothy Ryback in *Hitler's Private Library: The Books That Shaped His Life* thinks so. "We believe literary reading is an ennobling enterprise. The underlying assumption is that we are better people for reading." And yet what's shocking about Hitler is that "he read to fuel exactly the opposite, everything that was destructive to intellectual processes". His reading "was superficial ... vicious ... a gutter intellectualism".

Alberto Manguel prefers to think more positive thoughts. He opens his book with a quotation from Northrop Frye: "A big library really has the gift of tongues & vast potencies of telepathic communication." In such hallowed space, the dead speak to the living and the unborn. Who does Manguel read? With whom is he in "telepathic communication"? Classic authors for the most part, from Spanish, French and English literatures. Manguel reads broadly across cultures and time zones, in and out of several languages, much like his mentor Jorge Luis Borges did decades earlier. Borges occupies the highest perch in Manguel's personal library.

In *A History of Reading,* a treasure trove of delight and surprise, Manguel quotes Robert Louis Stevenson as saying that the classic writers "with whom we make enforced and often painful acquaintanceship at school ... pass into the blood and become native in the memory". Manguel's ongoing dialogue with Borges since his adolescent years has passed into his blood and is native in his memory.

Manguel talks about his reading aloud to the blind Borges on at least three occasions: briefly in "Borges in Love" from his essay collection *Into the Looking-Glass Wood,* briefly in *A History of Reading,* and at length in *With Borges.*

In *A History of Reading,* Manguel writes: "One afternoon ... Borges came to the bookstore accompanied by his eighty-eight-year-old mother ... He was almost completely blind ... and he would pass a hand over the shelves as if his fingers could see the titles. He was looking for books to help him study Anglo-Saxon ... he asked me if I was busy in the evenings because he needed (he said this very apologetically) someone to read to him ... I said I would." ["Borges in Love" says: "I accepted, unaware of the privilege."] "Over the next two years I read to Borges, as did many other fortunate and casual acquaintances."

In an interview with Clark M. Zlotchew in 1984 published in *Jorge Luis Borges: Conversations,* Borges describes his being read to: "Someone comes to visit me, and I ask him or her to read to me." He makes no mention of Manguel, or anyone else, as one of his readers. As Manguel notes in *A History of Reading,* "Borges chose the book, Borges stopped me or asked me to continue, Borges interrupted to comment, Borges allowed the words to come to him. I was invisible."

Borges' book selections often entailed 19th-century Americans such as Edgar Allan Poe and Mark Twain (poets Whitman and Dickinson, too) and the century-straddling colossus Henry James. The last time Manguel read to Borges, he read James' story "The Jolly Corner". Borges also adored the Victorian and Edwardian cadences of England, hence Manguel would often read (what Borges called his rereading) Kipling, Chesterton, Thomas De Quincey and Robert Louis Stevenson.

About Stevenson, in a 1982 interview with Donald Yates, Borges said, "I am always going back to Robert Louis Stevenson ... I admire everything in Stevenson. I admire the man, I admire the work, I admire his courage. I don't think he wrote a single indifferent or despicable line."

Summoned to read, Alberto Manguel in *A History of Reading* remembers being "led by the maid through a curtained entrance" to Borges who offered a "soft hand outstretched". He remembers sitting in an armchair, with Borges sitting "expectantly on the couch". He remembers the "slightly asthmatic voice" that would ask, "Shall we choose Kipling tonight? Eh?"

In *With Borges,* a volume the size of your hand and perfect for your pocket, Manguel remembers things with a different emphasis. He drops the asthmatic voice, the expectant waiting on the couch and the "Eh?" at the end of the question about Kipling. The sentence reads, "Well, shall we read Kipling tonight?"

Manguel fleshes in details about time and place: "For several years, from 1964 to 1968, I was fortunate enough to be among the many who read to Jorge Luis Borges. I worked after school in an Anglo-German bookstore of Buenos Aires, Pygmalion, where Borges was a frequent customer." He gives an account of the proprietor, Miss Lili Lebach, "a German woman who had escaped the Nazi horrors". He informs the reader that he was 16 at the time, a member of a fraternity of readers "whose identities are rarely known to one another but who collectively hold the memory of one of the world's great readers".

The tone of *With Borges* (I prefer the original title of *Reading to Borges*) is one of poignancy and loss. Manguel felt himself ill-equipped to remember all that he ought to have remembered. (To tweak Henry James a little: a youth is someone on whom almost everything is lost.) He constructs "a memory of a memory of a memory". He did not take notes at the time. The older man writing the memoir of his reading experience to a blind seer is too honest to alter the 16-year-old's inadequacy, to fatten or elongate a certain paucity into plenitude. He notes the boy's deficiencies and regrets them. There is a good deal of the Portuguese word *saudade* in *With Borges,* a longing and hunger for what might have been. And yet the book is not sentimental or nostalgic; it is much too unflinching for that.

There are times in Manguel's memoir when the boundary between biography and autobiography blurs. Boswell slips into Rousseau. "For Borges, the core of reality lay in books; reading books, writing books, talking about books." Manguel, too, has books as the core of his reality. He, too, is a reader and writer (my word order is deliberate here), a translator and compiler, and, in a very Borgesian twist, a maker of books about books and stories about stories. For both the elder and the younger man from Argentina, one suspects that "reading is a form of pantheism".

One suspects, too, that when Manguel as a young man moved to Canada he found more "monotheists" than "pantheists", more readers of a particular genre or school or author than eclectic "bookivores" like himself and Borges. Manguel seems to read and write more for pleasure than edification. Joy is at the heart of his work. Reading and writing are affairs of the whole body, and the one form of lovemaking does not differ much from the other. Both are aspects of an imaginative and sensual intelligence.

Books have at least two lives: what they are in themselves and what they lead to. *With Borges* is a beautiful remembrance of one of the seminal makers of literature in the 20th century, and it leads one back to Borges' work, particularly to his public lectures *Seven Nights* and *This Craft of Verse,* both delivered from memory. Borges, says Manguel, would rehearse his lectures "until every hesitancy, every apparent search for the right word, every happy turn of phrase [was] soundly rooted in his mind".

Manguel on occasion, like Borges, plays the roles of historian, biographer and critic. He may have been too young to appreciate the literary time bomb put in his lap as a boy, but over a lifetime the explosive has continued to detonate in his consciousness. Like his mentor, he writes fictional stories based on fact (*Stevenson under the Palm Trees*) and essays with fictional flavours (his essay on Che Guevera in *Into the Looking-Glass Wood,* where he notes that the CIA agent in charge of Che's body "suddenly began to suffer from asthma, as if he had inherited the dead man's malady"). Like the fox, Manguel knows many things. Like a centaur, he has many parts.

In a critique published in *The Observer* on Eliot Weinberger's arrangement of *Jorge Luis Borges – The Total Library: Non-Fiction 1922–86,* Manguel makes the case for the porous borders of Borges' work. "Borges," he writes, "strove to write from the point of view of the reader for whom the academic divisions into fiction, non-fiction and poetry ... are merely prejudices or conventions. He used these terminological assumptions to tell essays to the tune of 'once upon a time', to disguise stories as reviews or essays and to compose poems that were essay-like explorations or stories in sonnet form." Like teacher like student?

Manguel goes on to ask, "To what genre do texts such as 'The Wall and the Books', 'Borges and I' ... 'Ars Poetica' belong? Who can place into genre words like 'Time is the substance of which I am made. Time is a river that sweeps me along, but I am the river; it is a tiger that tears me apart, but I am the tiger; it is a fire that consumes me, but I am the fire'?" Are these lines fiction, non-fiction or poetry?

At times, Manguel's life as a reader and writer seems to be an extension of Borges, as if two lives are necessary to complete the passions and interests of one person's existence. Where their souls mate is in their fondness for the vast and the minute, for histories and footnotes. Manguel, both in his essay "Borges in Love" and in his novella *Stevenson under the Palm Trees,* quotes from a Borges favourite, Sir Thomas Browne's *Religio Medici,* that "men are liv'd over again" in a "revived self". Alberto Manguel has a Borgesian imagination: the universe is a book. When you open a page, you open a world.

In his *The Dictionary of Imaginary Places* – a very Borgesian book in its sweep across time and space and its love of fantasy coupled with the arcane and the esoteric – under the entry "Babel" Manguel borrows details from Borges' story "The Library of Babel", and broadens them. Babel's library houses "everything: the minutely detailed history of the future, the autobiographies of the archangels, a faithful catalogue of the library, thousands and thousands of false catalogues, the true story of every man's death, the translation of every book in all languages. Generation after generation of librarians wander through the library in an attempt to find the Book."

Manguel writes with Borges over his shoulder. In *The City of Words,* he recognizes that "no literary text is utterly original, … is completely unique, that it stems from previous texts, built on quotations and misquotations, on the vocabularies fashioned by others and transformed through imagination and use." He's happy to build his library, his books, his literary production, on the books of Borges. Maybe he remembers Susan Sontag's "letter" to Borges in *Where the Stress Falls:* "If books disappear, history will also disappear, and human beings will also disappear … Books are not only the arbitrary sum of our dreams, and our memory. They also give us the model of self-transcendence."

In the unadorned *With Borges,* the writing has the beauty and cadence of classical prose. The sentences dispense with frivolous and unnecessary descriptions and adjectives. The words have the strength of carefully chiselled stone. The book is small, like a Barbara Hepworth stringed sculpture, but its power and presence are no less imposing than a large Henry Moore bronze.

In his little book on Borges, in its fierce determination not to be exhaustive, not to tell all, nothing seems missing. It says the small; it shuns the large. Its smallness, its austerity, seem perfect.

III Robert Lax: Syllable and Word

D. H. Lawrence once wrote a short story called "The Man Who Loved Islands". Maybe it's the biography of Robert Lax, the man who hopped from island to island in the Aegean, changing houses more frequently than most people change cars and living off family inheritance and the kindness of strangers. One of his islands was Patmos, the island of visions and visionaries. Lax was a visionary too, living by an austere minimalism in all things. He lived within the colours of the Greek flag, blue and white, the blue sea and whitewashed houses, representing, according to myth, Aphrodite rising from seafoam. Maybe in the early years he went looking for love, but mostly he found a quiet place near the sea where he could do his work.

And what was his work? Writing, reading, drawing, doodling, walking, swimming, talking, dreaming ... These are the things he put an individual stamp on. He had 18 cats with whom he was intimate, who wandered in and out of his life. Maybe he modelled his behaviour on theirs: "They tend to get along with each other, whether or not they have a reason to ... They're light on their feet. They can remain motionless for such a long time." Lax had a light touch, he could remain motionless for a long time, he got along with others. Why Patmos? "No distractions. Excellent climate ... A fertile, unfolding quiet. Beautiful, inspiring light." He lived a solitary life, a monastic life.

Was he a saint? Maybe. If so, by not wanting to be, by not trying, by being himself. And what is a saint, Leonard Cohen's narrator asks in *Beautiful Losers*? "A saint is someone who has achieved a remote human possibility," the narrator answers himself. Like Lax, like Weil. "I think it has something to do with the energy of love."

When you enter into Robert Lax's world, you come to a place you may not have been to before. Or, maybe you come to the usual place but you see it differently. In *Thing 30* – Lax's words are things – he writes:

> be
>
> gin
>
> by
>
> be
>
> ing
>
> pa
>
> tient

Lax slows the world down. He slows it down by slowing down the means by which we filter and process the world: language. There is now a Slow Food movement. Lax was one of the originators of the Slow Language movement.

He was happy to be alive, happy to wake up and realize that the world hadn't eaten him. In *Box 16* – Lax's works were often stored in boxes – he celebrates aliveness:

what bliss

to

be

one

of

the

be

ings

His poems are little boxes of spirit and magic.

We are what we haunt, says André Breton in *Nadja*. We're also what we're haunted by. Robert Lax has a haunting presence to me, and to anyone who reads him attentively, anyone who incorporates something of Lax's life into his or her own. He searches, he waits: "… sometimes if you came, and I saw you, and I knew you were there, I'd continue to go on waiting." He respects the syllables, the slurps of sound. He sings the broken hallelujah, the fractured psalm.

There is a short story by the Swedish-born poet and novelist Lars Gustafsson that tells the tale of a young boy enclosed in his own sensual universe. The story is called "Greatness Strikes Where It Pleases". The boy is amazed at mushrooms for their soft-fluted underbellies and their strong earthy smells; he dreams a lot, he thinks, "The trees are so happy … when the wind comes. That gives them something to do." His brother and sister send him on errands. The world is a mystery to him and he is astonished by it. As he ages, he comes to know that he is "as slow as the galaxy and as mysterious". The story haunts me partly because I see a large part of Lax in it: the dreamer, the adorer, the praiser.

Lax wasn't mentally challenged as the boy in the story is; rather, he was a reader – by his window are stacks of books – an intellectual of sorts, an artist, but he shared the boy's infinite capacity to amuse himself with small things and small daily tasks.

According to Paul Spaeth, curator of the Robert Lax Archives at St. Bonaventure University in Olean, New York, Lax's first memory of himself as a maker of things occurred in early childhood. He "picked up a small flat stone and made a mark on it with another stone". He returned the marked stone to the ground with the thought that someone would eventually pick it up and know that another person had made the mark. This, he told Spaeth, was his earliest remembrance "of consciously creating a means of expression". In your imagination, you can picture the sculptural work of Andy Goldsworthy – his broken and coloured sticks or his broken and arranged stones – as visual analogues to Lax's split words in vertical columns.

Lax has his own way of writing where each word, each syllable, is given its just weight and fussed over as if it were an icon.

>   the look of the poem: i've always
>
>   liked the
>
>   idea of a poem or a word as a single
>
>   (arp-like image)
>
>   alone on a page
>
>   (an object of contemplation)

Alone on the page: that's what Lax does, he puts lone words and syllables on the page.

He incarnates the words of the poet Charles Wright: "One lives one's life in the word,/ One word and a syllable, word and one syllable."

One looks in vain for *Guernica*-like screeches and screams underneath Lax's happy exterior. He chose to tread lightly on the earth, chose not to take himself too seriously. His carbon footprint upon the earth is negligible. Some may be tempted to see him as a man of no account, to see his life as insignificant, and yet there is great bounty in his life. He gives of himself abundantly. He is one of the rare ones; he has the courage to be himself. He is open to the world, receptive to whatever heaven puts in his cup. He lives in wonder. He lives with thankfulness. The world is beautiful and holy to him.

Lax is the solitary who lives on islands, the poet who writes skinny poems, the Jew who converts to Catholicism, the Catholic who, in friend Jack Kerouac's words, is at the same time "a strange wonderful laughing Buddha". He is also the American who develops deep and long-lasting friendships. His friendship with Thomas Merton, sustained as much by letter as by personal contact, is one of the longest and deepest between two literary figures of the twentieth century.

Once Lax makes a friend, he keeps him – whether monk Merton or painter Ad Reinhardt or journalist Edward Rice or teacher Mark Van Doren. Lax approaches friendship reverently. In *Journal C* shortly after Merton's death and several years after Reinhardt's and other friends', Lax records this entry: "i remember the people i loved (who have died) or who've just disappeared – remember their traits as though it were a sacred duty." That is the way he remembers Merton in "Harpo's Progress" and "Remembering Thomas Merton and New York". He waits for

Merton in Patmos, not knowing that Merton will die from accidental electrocution in Bangkok before arriving.

He remains the one indispensable commentator on Merton's life and work, the one who sees the hidden wholeness and the integrated splinters, the one who connects the wholeness with holiness. To stay within a single letter of the alphabet, he sees how Merton's politics and prayers and pranks, his photography and poetry and philosophy are all interrelated. But one letter isn't really enough; you need a whole alphabet for a man as complex as Merton.

Lax conjures over 500 *things* in his career: single poems, pamphlets, journals, letters, graphic art, film, video, photography and performance art. About Lax, author William Maxwell writes: "If you placed him among the Old Testament figures above the south portal of Chartres, he wouldn't look odd." Kerouac describes him as "a Pilgrim in search of beautiful Innocence, writing lovingly, finding it, simply, in his own way." His Swiss German publisher, Pendo in Zurich, presents his writings bilingually, English on the left-hand page and German on the right-hand page. His publisher summarizes his life this way:

Robert Lax

born 1915
in Olean, N.Y. (USA):
studied at
Columbia University
editorial collaborator at
The New Yorker (1941),

Time magazine (1945),
Jubilee magazine (1953-1976);
lives since 1963 on the
Greek Islands Kalymnos
and Patmos

One important detail is missing. He died in his sleep on September 26, 2000, in Olean, New York. He was 84.

Of the islands where he spent most of his last forty years, Lax says this in a 1986 *New York Quarterly* interview: "I like being in a place where there is sea and sky and mountains, trees, even olive trees, and sheep and goats, shepherds. These are things which are natural, sacral, ancient ..." All these life forms are a necessary and vital part of his life.

You are what you lack. Lax lacks a wife and children. He has friends instead. Simone Weil lacks humour in her writing, although her brother maintains that she had it in life. She sees the world as neither funny nor absurd. She's intensity and conviction and steadfastness and absolutism. We measure how far we've fallen by her erect and courageous posture. Humourless: and in that respect very un-Jewish and even un-Christian in the medieval sense of the word. There is lots of humour in Robert Lax.

What there isn't in Lax is politics. As far as I can see, none at all. Not like his friend Thomas Merton in that respect. Merton, who died in 1968, spent a significant portion of his intellectual life putting into words Lawrence Ferlinghetti's 1988 oil painting, *Unfinished Flag of the United States,* where the blood-red stripes extend across the globe. The image speaks louder than a thousand words on America's appetite to destroy and devour, to spread its influence and control everywhere. Can you be apolitical? It wouldn't have mattered to

Lax what form of government was in power. He'd seek out the marginal people and spend time with them, seek out the circus performers, the vagabonds, the sponge divers.

He followed a circus troupe across western Canada for a year and wrote his best-known long poem about their performances and lives; it's called *Circus of the Sun.* He spent time with the poor and the unemployed in Marseille. He befriended fishermen and sponge divers on the Greek islands of Kalymnos and Patmos. His quintessential painting would be something like my friend Wayne Allan's installation, *Christ on the Road to Emmaus*: a plastic clown in a yellow box walking and waving with two fellow clowns. Or maybe Allan's box of Jesus playing baseball. A holy moment leavened by humour and playfulness. Lax's sense of the holy breaks into levity more frequently than into solemnity and seriousness. An exception is his relentlessly intense *21 Pages*.

You are what you're missing. There is no anger in Lax. Here again he differs from his more famous friend, Thomas Merton, whose merry mind had knives in it. Maybe you need a measure of anger for politics. While there's no politics in Lax there is loyalty, and there are letters, friendship, appreciation, quiet, poetry, drawings, observations, memory, awe, reverence, patience, conversations, long walks, swims, extended dreams …

slow
boat

calm
riv
er

qui

et

land

ing

When you read Lax's skinny poems, you pause, you reflect, you dream. Poet and critic Richard Kostelanetz says that Lax sought linguistic purity in the same way that his friend Ad Reinhardt sought it in the visual arts and his friend Thomas Merton sought it in spirituality. Certainly Reinhardt had an influence on Lax's writing: "Sometimes not specifically, but the general direction that he was working in certainly did – towards reducing the number of colours, reducing the form, and repeating the theme." The pure point of the poem was the single word or even the single syllable, "the unit of which poems are made".

Was Lax searching for the Ur-sound, the sound that began the universe, that began life? He sought greater and greater purification of his art to the point where the poem verged on disappearance the way a Giacometti sculpture threatens to disappear in its extreme thinness. He saw his art as "an extension, a development of life ... it is a further development of nature, a further refinement of processes already in existence".

In contrast to the Catholic Jewish thinker Simone Weil, he seems untroubled, unconflicted. One of the things Freud admired about dogs was that they were unconflicted. They were what they were, without questions and analysis. People are usually cankered with doubt, besotted by ambivalence.

Lax seems happy in his poetry, his letters, his drawings, his journal jottings, his friendships. Not self-conflicted. His art, in word and image, is almost always personal, directed to a particular person or composed for a particular person. That person was often his friend Merton, the Trappist monk. Lax seems at peace with the world and easy in his skin. Merton, in *The Seven Storey Mountain,* speaks of his friend as a kind of Hamlet, by which I think he means a questioner. (To me, Merton himself seems more closely tied to Hamlet in his incessant self-interrogation.) Lax is a kind of Elias, Merton says. "A potential prophet, but without rage. A king, but a Jew too. A mind full of tremendous and subtle intuitions … And the secret of his constant solidity I think has always been a kind of natural, instinctive spirituality, a kind of inborn direction to the living God." Lax's beautiful compliment to Merton was, "… I was most myself when I was with him."

Lax was loved by his parents. He was also loved by his sister and his extended family, including his niece Marcia, whom I had the pleasure of interviewing in Manhattan with my friend Michael Higgins. His conversion didn't seem to shatter the family bond. His mother did ask him to live within Judaism for a year as a practising Jew and to think carefully about his decision. His father wrote a beautifully supportive letter, but also asked that he "not convert any Jewish boys". My own feeling is that Merton's conversion to Catholicism had a great deal to do with Lax's. In other words, Lax's conversion to some extent was an act of solidarity with his best friend.

Lax continued to draw inspiration from the Prophets throughout his life, continued to immerse himself in Kabbalah. "The Hebrew word *kabbalah* has to do with receiving, how to better receive and perceive holy wisdom in the world," he tells S. T. Georgiou in *The Way of the Dreamcatcher: Spirit Lessons with*

Robert Lax: Poet, Peacemaker, Sage. Lax doesn't let go of things; he gathers them. He is at home in multiple religious traditions, including the Buddhist and the Native. His immediate roots were in Austria and Poland. "And I think it's been discovered that our family was of Sephardic Jewish ancestry, so the roots go back to Spain ... There are Laxes in Spain and Laxes even in Turkey ..." he says in conversation with Georgiou.

He writes a poem mindful of his heritage. The poem is playfully entitled "Shorter History of Western Civilization". The following words, thrust into a litany of names including Egyptians, Babylonians, Persians and Christians, are repeated like a mantra:

>
> Greeks &
>
> Jews
>
>
> Greeks &
>
> Jews

He omits the Chinese and the Arabs in the poem, but not in a journal entry from *Journal D* where he acknowledges: "to be a greek, as to be a jew, or an arab, or a chinaman/is to be quite an old thing." To some extent, Lax lived on his Greek islands as a Jew among Greeks, a Catholic among the Orthodox, a stranger in a community.

Epiphanies visit Thomas Merton in abundance. His life periodically trembles from Pauline blasts of light, whether in an old Cuban church in Havana, on the corner of Walnut and Fifth in Louisville, Kentucky, or by the Buddhist statues of Polonnaruwa in Sri Lanka. Simone Weil is also prone to dramatic turnings-around. She reads a poem by George Herbert and feels herself being physically gripped by Christ. Before this ultimate epiphany she experiences three lesser ones: Once entering a Portuguese village in "a wretched condition physically", she witnesses the wives of fishermen carrying candles and singing in procession around ships in a harbour. "There," she says, "the conviction was suddenly borne in upon me that Christianity is pre-eminently the religion of slaves, that slaves cannot help belonging to it, and I among others." Alone in Assisi, she avers, "(inside) the little twelfth-century Romanesque Chapel of Santa Maria degli Angeli, an incomparable marvel of purity where Saint Francis often used to pray, something stronger than I was compelled me for the first time to go down on my knees."

Edward Hirsch's poem "Simone Weil: In Assisi" gives high drama to this moment: "… something absolute/and omnivorous, something she neither believed/nor disbelieved, something she understood – /but what was it? – forced her to her knees." Then in Solesmes, France, at Easter, with a splitting headache, she finds "a pure and perfect joy in the unimaginable beauty of the chanting and the words". She understands for the first time divine love in the midst of affliction. The Passion of Christ enters into her head "once and for all".

Lax's spirituality seems quieter, calmer, less spectacular; it seems built by everyday occurrences in everyday experience. Small gestures, small rituals, small objects: these seem central to his spiritual life. "Prayer," Georgiou quotes him as saying, "is a way of sending out love in all directions." If he is who admirers say he is – a poet, a juggler, a holy acrobat, a drawer and doodler, a saint, a mystic, a journal keeper, a letter writer, a *luftmensch* –

he is these things naturally. He falls into grace. It's not something he aims at and hits.

Lax has no Revelation in his island life, but he has a series of important revelations. In his introduction to *Journal C* he writes:

> *when i left new york for greece i had hoped only to find a quiet place to live for a while and write some poems ... quiet. i thought i needed it for my work, as a photographer needs a dark room. quiet, a place to get away from people? bright light, loud noises and a constant presence of people (& of birds, goats, fish) is more the style. you are never alone in greece.*

He lived frugally on his savings and family money. He ate simply. He did his work: "ah, he likes to write, likes to get writing done, likes to get things on paper ..." he says to himself in the third person in *Journal C*. He breaks the day: "into discrete particles and puts them back together again. lets him know where he is & what he is doing, and prepares him for whatever new thing comes along. gets him ready with his cups and categories to contain whatever new thing <falls from heaven>." He wants to make a thing – that's what he calls his poems, they're things – "that will stand, a thing that will bear (that will sustain) repeated contemplation: a thing that will sustain long contemplation, and that will (in a <deep> enough way) reward the beholder." This is Lax recognizing both the physicality of his poetry and its spiritual durability. He doesn't refer to his work as either minimalist or concrete, as his critics do. Lax makes words. He breaks up language, breaks up words, and rearranges words in new ways so that the reader can, perhaps for the first time, both see and hear the words. He gives his work to friends. Some of his things get published. Some don't.

What Lax does a lot of in his island life is wait:

> the face of one
> waiting & waiting
>
> waiting & waiting
>
> waiting for a
> good he knows
> he cannot
> make

He waits in "holy receptivity". In this short poem, the repetition, the empty space, make the waiting real to the reader.

Both Judaism and Christianity are, according to novelist John Updike, religions shaped by waiting. Judaism waits for the Messiah. Christianity waits for the return of the Messiah. Jesus waits at the door.

Waiting is also the central part of Lax's masterpiece *21 Pages,* a work that belongs on the same shelf as Merton's *Hagia Sophia.* Lax's holy wisdom is to know that waiting and paying attention are forms of prayer. *21 Pages,* in the book *33 Poems* edited by Thomas Kellein, is an extended prayer, a prose poem, a deep meditation. In meditative prose, prayerful and poetic, the narrator waits for a god, an angel, a friend, himself. William Maxwell says this about the masterwork: "I don't know any religious writing that moves me as much or is as persuasive as the prose communication with the unseen, unknown, unanswering but felt fountain-source of his belief, which begins: 'Searching for you, but if there's no one, what am I searching for? Still you ..."'

This work of strange beauty reminds me a little of Samuel Beckett's *Waiting for Godot* or Simone Weil's short prose work *Prologue* and her collected thoughts called *Waiting for God,* and even Paul Tillich's sermon "Waiting" in *The Shaking of the Foundations*. But neither these works nor any others with which I'm familiar, with the possible exception of lines from Leonard Cohen, speak more secretly to the soul than Lax's prose poem. Cohen's prayers "Holy is Your Name" and "Not Knowing Where to Go" from *Book of Mercy* draw near to Lax's prayer. Cohen's lines – "Not knowing where to go, I go to you./Not knowing where to turn, I turn to you./Not knowing what to hold, I bind myself to you./Having lost my way, I make my way to you" – echo Lax's patience to wait.

To enter some works of art you need to take your shoes off, the way Merton took his shoes off in his approach to the Buddha statues of Polannaruwa. You need to bow your head. You need to fall on your knees. If you're lucky enough to find a copy of *21 Pages,* throw away analysis, criticism, your schooling, your prejudices, your opinions. Enter the pages as if you too had lost someone precious and didn't know where to find her. Enter the pages the way a child would enter an apple orchard for the first time or a barn full of animals for the first time. Prepared to wait, enter the pages, like the speaker, not knowing precisely for whom you're searching or why you're waiting. There is only the searching. There is only the waiting. The rest is not our business

Between waiting and longing the lives of human beings twist and turn. Between these two states, we find what is most human within us and what most fundamentally connects us to the divine. We wait for what we most long for; we wait for what we most need.

Read Lax's "the port was longing" from *Love Had a Compass* in conjunction with *21 Pages*.

A voice speaks rapidly in the prose poem (for the most part Lax speaks very slowly in his writing), and asks itself questions: "… Would I know you if I saw you?" Whatever the voice asks, there is no immediate answer forthcoming. More voice than personality, the speaker in *21 Pages* waits, for "… Some person, some moment, some atmosphere, that I'd recognize as very much mine …" The speaker waits because he was made: "to go on waiting. Made, put together, invented, born, for that single, singular purpose: to watch, to wait." The speaker seeks the "beloved … my sought-after-being, my remembered-one … the one I'd looked for, the one I'd sought without any clear idea of who he or she might be, of what he or she might look like …" This nameless, invisible one is "you". And the speaker confides, "A readiness to recognize you; that's all I've brought, that's what I bring to the encounter." The speaker has grown accustomed to waiting on corners, on benches, in forests, in parks. The speaker confesses to himself: "… sometimes if you came, and I saw you, and I knew you were there, I'd continue to go on waiting."

These lines continue to haunt me:

And back to nights of looking, outward and in; not knowing which way I'm looking, but waiting and looking. Back to the night-watch. Day-watch and night-watch. Dusk to dawn, dawn to dusk. Mid-day to midnight … I didn't give up because I couldn't. I didn't, because I was made to go on waiting. Made, put together, invented, born, for that single, singular purpose: to watch, to wait. There is no giving up on the thing you were made to do. There's no giving up on being who you are.

There are no lines elsewhere in Lax comparable to these. Nothing of this depth and intensity and beauty and pain. Lax the waiting one, Lax in heartbreaking longing, what the Portuguese enflesh in a word, *saudade,* the homesickness that can never be satisfied, the subject moving through time and space without hope of an object to feed the hunger or quench the thirst. *I hunger. I thirst. I wait.* So says Robert Lax, and in saying so, speaks for us all.

IV Notes on John Berger and Simone Weil

AT THE BACK OF MANY JOHN BERGER BOOKS, there is a quote by Susan Sontag: "John Berger writes about what is important ... In contemporary English letters he seems to me peerless; not since D. H. Lawrence has there been a writer who offers such attentiveness to the sensual world with responsiveness to the imperatives of conscience." Berger must be fond of the endorsement because he uses it so often.

Berger and Sontag are rebels with causes. On one occasion they wrote about the same person: Simone Weil. She was also a rebel with causes. Weil is (*is* is more fitting somehow than was) a thinker and activist in the world about whose life at least two great poems were written (Edward Hirsch's "Simone Weil: In Assisi" and Rowan Williams' "Simone Weil at Ashford").

In his writing, John Berger marries sensuality with morality, the glistening sheen of the world with its political underpinning. Art critic, drawer, storyteller, memoirist, sometimes poet, always Marxist, he praises the world and critiques it at the same time. I was once privileged to share writerly space with this praise-critic. In the Toronto journal *Brick* (Number 55, Fall 1996) his piece "Will It Be a Likeness?" led the issue and my "Silent Lamp: The Lives of Thomas Merton" followed.

One of Berger's strengths rests in his recognition that there is no one way of seeing things, or people. There is no one story that does justice to all. There are many stories. There are many ways, perspectives, points of view. Berger looks at the world in solidarity with the dispossessed and the unrecognized. He stands with migrant workers and the victims of war and globalization. He is, in Thomas Merton's words, "on the side of the people who are being burned, cut to pieces, tortured, held as hostages, gassed, ruined, destroyed."

In the last sentence of *Here Is Where We Meet: A Story of Crossing Paths,* Berger announces his credo: "All you have to know is whether you're lying or whether you're trying to tell the truth …" He tells the truth in so far as any one person can tell it. Simone Weil also tells the truth. Months before her death, Simone Weil saw a production of *King Lear.* She was struck by the Fool's truth. Fools in Shakespeare, she ruminated in a letter to her parents, belong to a class of people "who have fallen into the lowest degree of humiliation, far below beggary, and who are deprived not only of all social consideration but also … of the specific human dignity, reason itself – and these are the only people who, in fact, are able to tell the truth. All the others lie." All the others "attenuate, mitigate, soften, and veil the truth", even Kent and Cordelia. Is Simone Weil a kind of Holy Fool? Is John Berger? By holy I mean someone who has the courage to be who he or she is; by fool, I mean someone who has the courage to say what he or she sees without self-deception or trickery.

John Berger was born in London in 1926. He served in the British army from 1944 to 1946. His father was an army officer who trained to be an Anglican priest and became a financial advisor. His mother was the proprietor of a coffee shop. Even these details are hard to come by. Berger is reticent about his family, and reticent about his Jewish heritage, although one somehow senses that the moral vision of the Prophets, and the consolidation of that vision in Jesus, underpin his thoughts and actions as much as Marxian philosophy.

He has had two pivotal educational experiences: one with "European refugees from fascism – political, mostly Jewish refugees" from whom he learned "history in a continental sense, and about politics in a sense much wider than that of the public debates going on then in England"; and the second with older peasants in a village in the Alps from whom he learned "about nature, the land, the seasons and a set of priorities by which ... to live". He still lives and works in this French village in the Alps. He speaks fast. He writes slow sentences that make you slow down, sentences that seem calm and composed despite the frenzy and foment beneath them, as if a man standing atop a live volcano had all the time in the world to say what he needed to say. He rides a motorcycle.

What Berger says in the middle of *Here Is Where We Meet* is one of the best things I've ever read about style: "Style? A certain lightness. A sense of shame excluding certain actions or reactions. A certain proposition of elegance. The supposition that, despite everything, a melody can be looked for and sometimes found." He fuses lightness and elegance in his writing. His intensity doesn't show. He skips words leisurely into melody as you'd skip a stone on a rough sea.

In contrast to his spoken style of the BBC production of *Ways of Seeing* in which he moves frenetically, breathlessly, in staccato, his written style pauses, reflects, breathes. He allows the wind to blow among his sentences, leaving space between one thought and another. His pace is measured.

The personal and the political entwine for Berger. Even in the midst of a fierce attack on the policies of the Israeli government in a chapter called "Stones" from *Hold Everything Dear* – What a beautiful title! Berger is so very good at titles, his best *And Our Faces, My Heart, Brief As Photos* – when he is standing on Jerusalem's stony ground "like a figure in a dream" he acknowledges his ancestors in Poland, Galicia and the Austro-Hungarian Empire. He identifies with "the just cause and the pain of those whom the state of Israel ... are afflicting to a degree that is tragically totalitarian." The words that I have elided with my ellipsis are: "(and cousins of mine)". He stands with the other while acknowledging his own personal connection to the perpetrators of violence. He embraces the other and the surround of the self.

John Berger in *Photocopies* writes four pages on Simone Weil. The pages are attentive and responsive, sensual and moral. Susan Sontag writes two pages on Simone Weil in *Against Interpretation*. Sontag's two pages on Weil are among the densest, deepest and most complex of her writing career. Weil once wrote that "Every human being cries out silently to be read differently." Berger reads her differently and Sontag does the same.

Sontag says that Weil is important; she has the air of authority, although it's an unhealthy authority. Weil is driven by the imperatives of her conscience; she is not appreciative of the sensual world. She cradles a "violently unfair hatred of Roman civilization and the Jews". She has "contempt for pleasure and for happiness"; she makes "noble and ridiculous political gestures", she self-denies elaborately; she tirelessly courts affliction. In appearance, she makes an impression by "her homeliness, her physical clumsiness, her migraines, her tuberculosis". I liken her to Catherine Tekakwitha in Leonard Cohen's novel *Beautiful Losers*. Like Tekakwitha, Weil is a severe ascetic and an absolutist, and yet there is something magnetically compelling about her authenticity.

Michael Higgins in his CBC *Ideas* broadcast in January, 1984 speaks of her life as being "extreme, intense, harried and searing ... a life of utter integrity and ravaged purity". She speaks to the broken parts of the world, to the broken people, to the broken parts of herself. If there is trouble, she goes to it. If there is pain, she's in the midst of it. From her heights we sense how far we've fallen. She gives herself away; we vainly strive to protect and defend the little container we call self.

Most of human life, Weil writes in her brilliant essay "*The Iliad,* or the Poem of Force*"*, "takes place far from hot baths". She goes to where pain is – the Spanish Civil War – or where drudgery is – a Renault factory – and she links hands with those who suffer. David Anderson astutely observes in his little book, *Simone Weil,* that when "she wrote about the crucifixion, she was not reflecting upon a theological doctrine: she was objectifying and transcending the affliction of her own soul and body", and the affliction of the souls and bodies of others. She swallows pain and spits it out. Her pain she can bear; the pain of others she can't. As someone we'd likely classify as an anorexic, she frequently employs oral metaphors. References to eating, drinking, swallowing, ingesting and digesting abound. If the words of Jesus in Matthew are true, and I believe they are, then she is blessed. She is blessed because she is among those who hunger and thirst for righteousness and justice.

A single sentence in Weil carries enormous weight of thought and great lightness of expression. "No poetry concerning the people is authentic if fatigue does not figure in it, and the hunger and thirst which come from fatigue." Maybe not since Pascal has a French writer written with more aphoristic terseness, with more blood and bone. Thought passes through her flesh into worded deeds.

One can imagine Weil writing sentences, maybe even chapters, in Sontag's *Illness as Metaphor, Aids and Its Metaphors,* and especially *Regarding the Pain of Others.* One can't imagine Sontag writing anything in Weil, so different are the sensibilities, and yet Sontag sees Weil with surprising clarity.

Weil, says Sontag, stands with "the presence of mystery in the world", a mystery that "the secure possession of the truth, an objective truth, denies". "In this sense," Sontag concludes, "all truth is superficial; and some (but not all) distortions of the truth, some (but not all) insanity, some (but not all) unhealthiness, some (but not all) denials of life are truth-giving, sanity-producing, health-creating, and life-enhancing." Sontag hints that Weil's personal distortion, insanity and denial contribute to the truth, sanity and health of the whole.

Robert Coles in his *Simone Weil: A Modern Pilgrimage* makes the claim that Weil rejected the healthiness of Judaism. Because, for her, sickness was more real?

> *She may have known full well that Judaism is a religion of this earth, a religion which takes open and honest stock of the here and now and urges its adherents to engage themselves in that here and now fully and vigorously, as honorably as their ability allows them to. Judaism is not a penitential religion or an immediately messianic one; it dedicates itself to each day's, each year's personal and ethical responsibilities ... the point is not prolonged suffering, self-flagellation, a life of abstinence or restriction – themes which have attended Christianity all along. The Jewish faith and the Jewish culture, for all the suffering Israel's people have experienced over the centuries, the*

millennia, is on the whole a lusty, joyous faith, solidly affirming of the life we have.

John Berger says nothing of Weil's Jewishness, or her Jewish self-denial. About her complexities, her paradoxes, her self-destruction, he says simply, in exaggerated understatement, "She was disconcerting, no question." Weil died on August 24, 1943, in a sanatorium in Kent, "having deliberately restricted her intake of food to the rations inflicted on her compatriots in occupied France".

Weil's Jewishness is problematic, to use that popular word in postmodern discourse. In application for a teaching post, she writes a letter to the ministry of education in the Vichy government in November, 1940, six months after France had fallen to the Nazis. She writes in an atmosphere of anti-Semitic documents, including "the Statutory Regulation on Jews". She writes to deny, and disown, her Jewishness. In a legalistic and contorted Jesuitical parsing of language, she claims not to know the definition of the word Jew since "the subject has never been part of my program of studies". She has never been to a synagogue (she attends a synagogue for the first time in New York City, a congregation of Ethiopian Jews), never witnessed a Jewish religious ceremony. Her parents were freethinkers. She makes no mention of her father, a family physician, being able to read Hebrew and write Hebrew poetry.

The statutory regulation defines a Jew as someone with three or more Jewish grandparents. Weil says that she has only two Jewish grandparents, so on that basis she can't be Jewish by the criteria of the regulation. Furthermore, she argues that the Romans massacred the Jewish population in Jerusalem. The survivors were transported as slaves, and the majority of the slaves perished in the circuses. Only the Jews living outside of Palestine could have had descendants. Her ancestors, however, came from Alsace on her father's side; "... no family tradition, to my knowledge, tells us whether they arrived in distant times from some other country." Prior to France, her mother's family "lived ... in a country with a Slavic population, and nothing leads me to suppose that it was composed of any group but Slavs".

If I understand her argument, she is not a Jew because she has only two Jewish grandparents; she is not a Jew because she has never been to a synagogue; she's not a Jew because her parents are freethinkers, and she's not a Jew because there is no agreed-upon definition of the word. There are no Jews anyway, because they perished in Palestine, and if there are Jews, they were dispersed to Jewish communities in Europe. Since her mother and father's families didn't live in Jewish communities, they weren't Jews and neither is she.

Weil's biographer, Simone Petrement, in *Simone Weil: A Life*, puts forward the proposition that Weil's letter doesn't mean she wasn't "in solidarity with other Jews". Petrement further argues that Weil's arguments "in regard to race were valuable for all Jews". She was merely mocking the "Statutory Regulations on Jews" and "the confused ideas on which all anti-Semitic racism rests". According to Petrement, Weil's letter doesn't mean what it appears to mean.

Anna Freud in conversation with Robert Coles says, "I don't for a moment think that she ever convinced herself that she wasn't Jewish ..." She wasn't, however, according to Anna Freud, simply taunting the authorities, "making fun of them with her superior intelligence and knowledge and ability to phrase things. She wanted to believe what she wrote but didn't." If she wouldn't accept the word Jew as part of her self-definition, then others would affix the appellation to her. Her friends in the south of France regarded her as Jewish; she was denied her request to be parachuted behind German lines to do undercover work because she looked so stereotypically Jewish.

The conclusion of Weil's letter to Vichy educational authorities is unambiguously clear: "The Christian, French, Hellenic tradition is mine; the Hebrew tradition is foreign to me; no text of a law can change that for me." In an interview with Robert Enright in *Border Crossings* (Spring, 1995), Berger sounds like Weil: "... I'm deeply a traditionalist in my imagination. The text which means so much to me is the Bible, particularly the New Testament and the Greeks."

Berger's and Weil's positions may not be as radical as they sound. Jewish-Italian novelist and Holocaust survivor Primo Levi, in his chapter "The Intellectual in Auschwitz" from *The Drowned and the Saved,* remembers a particular Jewish thinker in the Camp who did not consider himself to be a Jew because he had no awareness of Jewish tradition. He refused to assume an identity that didn't belong to him. "Whoever was not born within the Jewish tradition is not a Jew and cannot easily become one," Levi empathetically asserts. Hannah Arendt once remarked, "I did not know from my family that I was Jewish ... The word 'Jew' never came up when I was a small child." Arendt's Jewishness was forged by others: "I first met up with it through anti-Semitic remarks ... from children on the street. After that I was, so to speak, 'enlightened'."

I don't know to what extent irony plays a part in Weil's letter. She is too unrelentingly clear in her mind and in her prose not to be aware of the letter's flaws and contradictions. She doesn't sound ironic, although in a subsequent letter to Xavier Vallat, Commissioner of Jewish Affairs, irony has a forceful presence.

Weil, with her tongue in her cheek, thanks him for being partly responsible for rejecting her teaching application and enabling her to take up a position as a grape cutter on a grape farm. She writes scaldingly: "I consider the statute concerning the Jews in a general way as being unjust and absurd, for how can one believe that a university graduate in mathematics could harm children who study geometry by the mere fact that three of his grandparents attended a synagogue?" Weil informs the commissioner that she is doing well on the farm. Her employer has complimented her that even though she is a city girl she might still marry a farmer. "He does not know, it is true, that simply because of my name I have an original defect that it would be inhuman for me to transmit to children."

Like Jacob, Weil wrestles with an angel, a Jewish angel. She doesn't, however, seek a blessing; she seeks release. Her brother, André, a brilliant mathematician, in conversation with Malcolm Muggeridge in *Gateway to God,* a British collection of his sister's writings, vouches for the "non-Jewishness" of their family: "... I even remember that during the war someone told me I was Jewish and I just didn't know what that meant. This is something that could not happen in the modern world ..." Her brother implies in the interview that during the pre-war years a Jew could define himself as he pleased. After the war, after the Holocaust, a Jew was defined by gentiles. His thinking seems to parallel Jean-Paul Sartre's that a Jew is somebody whom others regard as Jewish.

Is there a single unambiguously positive sentence about Jews or Judaism in the whole of Weil's writing? Even when she specifies particular meritorious books of the Old Testament in her "Letter to a Priest" – "Isaiah, Job, the Song of Solomon, Daniel, Tobias, part of Ezekiel, part of the Psalms, part of the Books of Wisdom, the beginning of Genesis ..." (quite a large portion of the Hebrew

Bible!) – she does so in the context of their being assimilated "by a Christian soul". "The rest is indigestible, because it is lacking in an essential truth which lies at the heart of Christianity and which the Greeks understood perfectly well – namely, the possibility of the innocent suffering affliction."

On the other hand (you need three or four hands when dealing with Weil), she unequivocally opposes Hitler:

Ever since the day when I decided, after a very painful inner struggle, that in spite of my pacifist inclinations it had become an overriding obligation in my eyes to work for Hitler's destruction ... my resolve has not altered; and that day was the one on which Hitler entered Prague – in May 1939 ... My decision was tardy ... and I bitterly reproach myself for it.

She supports the French resistance. Yet her statements about Jewish theology are overwhelmingly negative. In a sentence: "The twofold Hebraic and Roman tradition has in great measure negated, for two thousand years, the divine inspiration of Christianity." It seems as if Weil could only believe in a wounded God, a suffering God. The all-powerful deity of the Hebrew Bible was repugnant to her, as was the all-powerful Roman state. The Archbishop of Canterbury, Rowan Williams, in "Simone Weil at Ashford", puts words to her emaciated flesh: "... and if I cannot walk like god,/ at least I can be light and hungry, hollowing my guts/ till I'm a bone the sentenced god can whistle through."

Yet it is also true, as Francine du Plessix Gray asserts in her Penguin Lives biography, *Simone Weil*, that Weil's "thinking and her personality had a deep kinship with the Jewish tradition". "There is her love of polemic; her penchant for Talmudically hair-splitting judgments; her tendency to rhetorical extremes; stern emphasis on an absolute obedience to God's will; the pessimistic panache ..."

John Berger calls his chapter, his mini-essay on Simone Weil, "A Girl like Antigone" in recognition of Weil's stand for justice. He begins with a description of her table. It's 80 cm x 200 cm. It's probably made of pearwood. On the table she has a functional lamp. "The table is in the room where she worked and slept when she was at home." In her "vagrant life", she probably spent more time reading and writing on this table than on any other table.

Moving on from the description of the table, Berger quickly enters the personal. He says that he's looked at many photographs of Weil. He once drew a portrait of her from a photograph. Drawing her makes her familiar to him. It's as if he met her. She inspires, he says, "... a physical antipathy, a sense of my own inadequacy, a certain exhilaration at the opportunity she appeared to offer of loving." In Plato, Berger suggests, poverty is love's mother.

Near the close of his meditation on Weil's short life of thirty-four years, he returns to her table on the sixth floor of the apartment on Rue Auguste Comte where, when writing, she could see the rooftops of Paris. In a single sentence he captures the unity of her conflicting tensions with the insertion of a conjunction: "She loved the view from the window, and she was deeply suspicious of its privilege." The word *and* holds the tension and reintegrates the splitting of love and shame. They belong together.

On a previous occasion Berger made similar use of the *and*. I'm quoting from memory. He said once about a farmer in his French village that the man loved his pig and ate his pig. *And* joins, it honours; it doesn't resolve or excuse. You can love a pig and eat it. You can love a window and feel ashamed for having a privilege that many are denied. *But* is a different kind of conjunction. It qualifies, prioritizes. Berger prefers *and;* he prefers it stylistically and morally.

Towards the end of his meditation – which is usually Berger's best form of writing, whether in his art criticism or his brief narratives or his polemics – Berger leaps. He leaps from description and fact and verifiable observation into identification and fusion. He claims that when Weil had a pen in hand, "… she returned in her mind to this table in order to begin thinking." Then she would forget the table. There is no way of Berger knowing this. This is him diving into another consciousness, into another being. This is him taking extreme risks – the possibility that he's simply wrong in his violation of her personhood. "If you ask me how I know this," he tells the reader, "I have no answer."

Berger enters Simone Weil's apartment, her room, her table. He sits at her table and reads her watershed poem. The sonnet is by George Herbert and it's called "Love". Weil copied it in English in "her hieroglyphic handwriting" and learned it by heart. When she is overcome by pain, she recites it "out loud, like a prayer". Once, when she is reading the poem, before she learns to recite it, she feels "the physical presence of Christ".

She isn't one to be moved by miracles, not even the ones in the New Testament. She doesn't believe in mysticism; she isn't a mystic. If anything, she is frequently an annoying and legalistic rationalist. She feels Christ gripping her. Her imagination plays no part in the experience, nor do her senses. She simply feels "across the pain, the presence of love, similar to that which one can read in a smile on a loved face".

In his penultimate paragraph, Berger makes a second leap, another jump across boundaries, another risk in dissolving the normal categories of reason. During the time it takes for him to read Herbert's poem, the poem becomes "a place, a dwelling".

There is nobody in the dwelling, Berger says. The dwelling is "shaped like a stone beehive". He informs his reader that there are "tombs and shelters like this in the Sahara". He says that he has read many poems in his life, but none, before now, has he visited. "The words were the stones of a habitation which surrounded me." I don't know what to make of his words, but they may have some connection to one of Berger's most famous sentences: "The number of lives that enter any one life is incalculable." Simone Weil's life has entered his.

Berger returns to fact, to the everyday world, in his concluding paragraph. He informs his reader that the entrance to Weil's apartment block, which you need a code to get into, has a plaque that reads: "Simone Weil, philosopher, lived here between 1926 and 1942." Sometimes the French are good at simplicity and transplanted Englishmen know well enough to leave their plainspokenness alone.

V Muriel Rukeyser: In Each Word a Storm

A POEM CALLS TO YOU if you bend your ear to it. "A Little Stone in the Middle of the Road, in Florida", for instance. A charming title. Itself a poem.

> My son as a child saying
> God
> is anything, even a little stone in the middle of the road, in
>   Florida.
> Yesterday
> Nancy, my friend, after long illness:
> You know what can lift me up, take me right out of
> despair?
> No, what?
> Anything.

So much depends on that word *anything,* first clustered in a group, then breathing free and alone. Anything. Anything can happen, anything can change, God can come, despair can lift. The little boy's anything and the woman's anything. Word-chimes. Between anything and anything, a lot can happen.

Anything is a word at work in Muriel Rukeyser. Even when you don't see it or hear it in an individual poem, it's an informing foundation. Other essential words in her word-pool are *child, woman, Orpheus, suicide, song, touch, speak, you.* From words like these she builds her 593 pages of *Collected Poems.*

Do you need a poet and poem to line your pocket? Like a lucky penny. My parents thought so. Mother had Yeats and his "Lake Isle of Innisfree". She learned the poem by heart at age nine and never forgot it. Father had Wordsworth and his "Intimations of Immortality". For Dad, there was no higher calling in the world than the call to be a poet. He read theology, history and biography, but poetry was for him the highest ordering of words. I don't have a specific poem or poet in my pocket. In some moods, Muriel Rukeyser or Emily Dickinson. In others, Raymond Carver, Dennis Lee, Denise Levertov, Edward Hirsch, Robert Lax (I include his journals as part of his poetry) or early William Carlos Williams, and even a few poems by John Berger.

Tonight I'm thinking of Muriel Rukeyser and her "Despisals", maybe even her "Speed of Darkness" and "Effort at Speech Between Two People". I need to consider "Tree", "Kathe Kollwitz", "The Conjugation of the Paramecium", "Poem", "Islands", "The Gates", "Double Ode" and "Haying Before Storm", too. A poet only needs ten good poems to be a poet, and one or two great ones to be in the circle of Wordsworth. Rukeyser has "a storm in each word". She makes magic "of forgotten things".

I came to Rukeyser by way of her prose. This sentence caught my attention: "There is also, in any history, the buried, the wasted, and the lost." The sentence provided a way of seeing history, large and small. Aren't we what we've buried, wasted and lost?

Doesn't poetry, as in John Berger's introduction to his *Pages of the Wound,* speak of things that are no longer here – "[l]ike the dress, the shoes kicked off and the hairbrush".

The strange prose of *The Life of Poetry,* with its spaces and silences and leaps: I liked the way Rukeyser's mind moved. It reminded me a little of how the Brazilian storyteller Clarice Lispector's mind moved. Lispector, too, is concerned with seeing. Rukeyser's words might be Lispector's: "What do we see? What do we not see?"

The first poem to make an impression on me was "Despisals", which I read in an *Antaeus* anthology years ago. "Effort at Speech Between Two People", a poem I came to more recently, also made a strong impression. "Despisals" is late in Rukeyser's production, "Effort at Speech …" is early, one of her first published poems. "Effort at Speech …" reminds me of a style of speaking I trapped for a time – or, a style that allowed itself to be trapped – like a wind in a jar, but the wind soon blew open the jar. The style was uncontainable and irretrievable. I never got it back. My story was called "Kasaala", a fictionalized account of my days and nights in Africa when I was twenty-one.

Is that what draws me to Rukeyser? Her voice. What she leaves out. How her mind works. How the wind comes in. Words are hard to make – hard to say – in Rukeyser. She's not going to lie to you. In *The Life of Poetry* she says there are two essential American poetries: the poetry of outrage (Melville) and the poetry of possibility (Whitman). Rukeyser's is mostly a poetry of possibility, occasionally a poetry of outrage. Even in her politics, in her political poems, there is a sense of the primacy of making, of the need to make and build while you knock down and criticize. Listen to her in "Wherever":

Wherever
we walk
we will make

Wherever
we protest
we will go planting

Make poems
seed grass
feed a child growing
build a house

Whatever we stand against
We will stand feeding and seeding

Wherever
I walk
I will make

Even in a revolution, you need to seed and feed and build.

 I have forty or so anthologies of poetry in my library. Two or three have Muriel Rukeyser in them, including her two-poem presence in Harold Bloom's *American Religious Poems*. How quickly things change. You're a name for a few years, then students have a hard time finding you in the public library. If you're lucky, you come back later. Another generation digs you up. If you're unlucky, you stay buried. Rukeyser has one book of criticism on her work, a recent biography, and is the subject of a recent collection of remembrances and critical reappraisals; she doesn't seem much written-about in the journals. You could take a course in American poetry and not hear her name.

In a poem she seems to have written in response to a friend's suicide, she tells the reader to flower. Flower for the dead. The poem is called "The Power of Suicide".

> The potflower on the windowsill says to me
> In words that are green-edged red leaves:
> Flower flower flower flower
> Today for the sake of all the dead. Burst into flower.

Maybe if Rukeyser knew that many of her books were out of print, including her *Collected Poems,* the message would be the same. Flower. Just flower. (I'm sounding like a Nike commercial.)

In her personal essay "The Education of a Poet" Rukeyser says, "There were no books in the beginning..." Only Shakespeare and the Bible, the book of books. Her early days were not book-ended. Later, yes.

She doesn't tell you much about herself, a detail here and there, nothing too personal; she doesn't give much of her personal story away. You learn from others that she was probably bisexual, she had a son from a father different from the man she was married to for a few months, her favourite ice cream was Haagen Dazs' rum raisin. One of her last acts was to accept an invitation from the Modern Language Association to speak on

"Lesbians and Literature". Illness prevented her from going to speak. Rukeyser tells you some things in "Effort at Speech ..." Her widowed aunt played Chopin; on her birthday, after hearing a story about a dead rabbit she crawled under her chair and stayed there for a long while; she contemplated suicide at fourteen. There is more untold than told in Rukeyser. As a teacher, Rukeyser had this standard assignment: Complete this sentence "I could not tell ..." There was much Rukeyser chose not to tell, but she believed, according to her student Jane Cooper, that in what you cannot tell lie the inescapable poems. The necessary ones. The ones that have a will of their own and insist on an outing.

Her mother passed on her belief in a Jewish ancestor (Rabbi Akiba) who stood against the Romans and preserved the Song of Songs. "Resist the Romans," Rukeyser says in a poem. She could be Simone Weil speaking. "The holy poem .../ the Song of Songs always," she says in the same poem, in voice and conviction so very unlike Weil. Her father too is a strong presence in her poetry. He wants her to be a golfer. Instead she writes poetry (more rebellion) and protests injustices against blacks and workers and the Vietnamese. He's a cement salesman; he, in his daughter's eyes, helps to build New York City. Did her first thoughts on the need for form in poetry come from her having watched the pouring of cement into frames?

In the early years Rukeyser has a friend who says she won't talk to her anymore unless she stops constantly writing poems. Muriel promises her friend that she'll stop. She doesn't; she breaks her promise, goes on writing poems. Her father told her never to break a promise, and she feels very guilty at having done so. Rukeyser repeats this story in *The Life of Poetry*. It is her birth story. What should you call her? Jew? American? Poet? Poet first, poet before anything else. Even a poet in her Jewishness: "To be a Jew in the twentieth century/ Is to be offered a gift .../ The gift is torment." She decided to be a poet, even at the cost of friendship. She'd pay the price. She says in "The Speed of Darkness", as if speaking directly to her son: "I bastard mother/ promise you/ there are many ways to be born./ They all come forth/ in their own grace." Was she birthed by a broken promise?

The mother and father don't appear to be very happy in Rukeyser's work – not from what she says about them, but from what she doesn't say. You wonder if she came from a family like Delmore Schwartz's – long silences, tension, little physical contact. In "Dreams Begin Responsibilities" Schwartz's father does not take responsibility for his dreams of marriage and children. Rukeyser's family disinherited her. She felt herself to be untouched as a child. Did Rukeyser's parents take responsibility for their dreams?

Touch is important in Rukeyser's poetry. There are exhortations everywhere in the poetry to touch. She yearns for touch. Didn't her mother touch her? Is it possible to spend your whole life looking for what you missed in the first years of life? In "Islands", a sharp-edged little poem, Rukeyser makes a distinction between nature in general and human beings in particular as an odd concoction of nature: even islands are connected, while people remain distant.

> O for God's sake
> they are connected
> underneath

They look at each other
across the glittering sea
some keep a low profile

Some are cliffs
The bathers think
islands are separate like them

There are things you can't talk about in Rukeyser's family. In "The Education of a Poet", she says that in her family you couldn't talk about sex, money or death. She says in a poem that you can't talk about cock and cunt. In "Despisals", Rukeyser says not to despise the clitoris; in "The Speed of Darkness" she says: "Whoever despises the cunt despises the life of the child."

She quotes an analyst: "What you are dominated by in your childhood is whatever your parents really love." Is the reverse also true: what you are dominated by in your childhood is whatever your parents really despised and were afraid of? "Pay attention to what they tell you to forget," Rukeyser advises in a poem, and repeats the line three times. "Write poems out of the experiences that have eaten you," Rukeyser is quoted as saying in Sharon Olds' "A Student Memoir of Muriel Rukeyser".

Does one of her strongest poems, "Despisals", come out of rebellion against what her parents despised? Don't despise the ghetto, she says. Don't despise the Jew. The black. Sexuality. The homosexual. Don't despise touch. Don't despise the asshole. Don't despise the clitoris.

> ... Not to despise the other.
>
> Not to despise the *it*. To make this relation
>
> with the it : to know that I am it.

Here in three lines Rukeyser summarizes a core of Clarice Lispector's writing, about not despising the cockroach, about not despising our animal nature, about not despising the *it*.

In "Double Ode", one of her last poems, Rukeyser says: "Tonight I will try again for the music of truth." She's going to do it tonight. There's a sense of urgency. She's going to try again as if she's tried many previous nights in the past. She's going to try for the music of truth. Not the facts of truth, the objectivity of truth, the geometry of truth, but the music of truth. Truth comes in sound; it comes in finding the courage to say the real words, the words that don't cover up. It's one of her most beautiful lines: "Tonight I will try again for the music of truth." The truth is unattainable, but you go on trying, you go on flowering or trying to flower.

"The universe is made of stories,/ not of atoms" she proclaims in "The Speed of Darkness". If that's the case, how vital then is the need to tell the truth, to tell true stories.

"The building music," she says in another poem. You build words, you build music, you build truth.

> Tonight I will try again for the music of truth.
>
> ...
>
> Moving toward new form I am –
>
> ...
>
> Do I move toward form, do I use all my fears?

She touches me here. Her looking for a form in "Double Ode" is me looking for a form. I've searched a long time for a form that would allow me to join things in a certain way and to play with them and even pray with them. What I take from her words is to use everything, the whole body, the whole person, not to waste, not to bury, not to lose.

Things are not easy for Muriel Rukeyser. Things are not easily said. When I read a poem whose author is unknown to me, I say, could this be Rukeyser? If the words seem easily said, I know it's not. If they seem said with great difficulty, I nod to myself yes, this could be Rukeyser. Speech is an effort, writing is an effort. In an "Effort at Speech Between Two People" she writes:

> Speak to me. Take my hand. What are you now?
> I will tell you all.   I will conceal nothing.
> ...
> Oh, grow to know me. I am not happy. I will be open:
> ...
> Speak to me. Take my hand. What are you now?

Isn't this speech too intimate for poetry? Too naked for form? It's a cry, not a poem. Not art, but pain. A desperate lunge towards the other, even if the other isn't there or there is no other. Hands. Words. Me. You. The need for conversation, the need for touch, the need for the other. I will tell you everything (no, I won't). I will conceal nothing (I will conceal almost everything). I am unhappy (yes, that's true). I will be open (no, I won't).

Some of the lines are true, some are untrue. But there is music in them all. "What would happen if one woman told the truth about her life?" Rukeyser asks in her poem "Kathe Kollwitz". She answers her own question: "The world would split open." To keep the world from splitting, she doesn't tell the truth.

There comes a time in a poet's career where there is a new turning, "a directer relation with the sun" says Thoreau. "The turning", as it's called in Heidegger. "A New Path to the Waterfall" Raymond Carver calls it. There's a change in diction, a gathering of energies, a moment when the self seems to find itself or speak itself.

Emily Dickinson is struck by lightning in poem 1581, and the lightning "Struck no one but myself –/ But I would not exchange the Bolt/ For all the rest of Life –". She writes the poem in 1883, the year of her great poetic outpouring. It doesn't differ in diction or in style from the poems before it or after it, but it gives voice to a singular event that transformed, or made her fully conscious of, her writing life. Critics argue over watershed poems. Is it this one? Is it that one? I think it's the lightning poem in Dickinson, the first time she enfleshes a metaphor to do justice to her precarious mental state and her overpowering strength to record it.

I don't know. How can one be sure? All I know is that when I read the Dickinson lightning poem I feel the lightning, feel the force of direct truth-telling instead of her more usual slanted speech. But because I'm cleaved by the bolt, does that mean the poet is too? Does she receive the same electric charge in her writing as I do in my reading?

Is there a transformative turn-around poem for Rukeyser? I think there is. The year of publication is 1958, the book is *Body of Waking,* the poem is "Haying Before Storm".

The sky is unmistakable. Not lurid, not low, not black.
Illuminated and bruise-color, limitless, to the noon
Full of its floods to come. Under it, field, wheels, and
    mountain,
The valley scattered with friends, gathering in
Live-colored harvest, filling their arms; not seeming to hope
Not seeming to dread, doing.
                      I stand where I can see
Holding a small pitcher, coming in toward
    The doers and the day.
                      These images are all
    Themselves emerging: they face their moment: love or go
down.
    A blade of the strong hay stands like light before me.
    The sky is a torment on our eyes, the sky
    Will not wait for this golden, it will not wait for form.
    There is hardly a moment to stand before the storm.
    There is hardly time to lay hand to the great earth.
    Or time to tell again what power shines past storm.

I don't know the context for this poem, what it leads out of or leads into. I don't know its compositional history, whether it came fast or slow, whether the final draft is different from the first. I just have the words in front of me and they go straight into the bloodstream. This for me is Rukeyser's lightning poem. A storm. That can't be described, or can only be described in negatives. It's not this, not that. The harvesters can't be described either;

they're not this, not that. The storm is. The harvesters do. Being and doing: the two interactive states of human consciousness and perhaps the two interactive states between what is there and who we are – we that part of Being not content to be.

The poet tells this short tale of a gathering storm with herself standing where she can see. She's the observer. Neither a part of the sky nor the people working under the sky. She carries a pitcher. Presumably water for the workers on a hot day at noon, on a day about to change drastically. Images emerge from the poet's consciousness as if she's in a dream or a trance or a dream-trance. She sees a single blade of golden and the tormenting sky. Something is going to happen. There will be no waiting for gold or form. Time is running out. There's hardly time to stand or touch or tell. Hardly time. But there is time enough. Time enough to stand, to touch and to tell. First you have to feel the outrage of deprivation. Then you can more fully appreciate the possibility of replenishment. The good must be taken away, or the threat must be there that it may be taken away, before it can be given back. Before you can say again there's a power shining past storm, a power deeper and stronger than storm.

This to me is a poem of faith and hope, but only at the articulated cusp of absolute loss, at the risk of utter deprivation and devastation. You can't get to the shining power any other way. You need a storm to see it and feel it and articulate it. You need *a storm in each word* to approach it.

VI Leonard Cohen and the Power of the Strange

A STREAK OF STRANGENESS runs through a work of quality and durability. So argues literary critic Harold Bloom. The strangeness keeps the work from staleness, constantly refreshing images and rejuvenating words. Leonard Cohen has lines that, once you read them and take them to heart, you never forget – lines such as "Dance me through the panic/ till I'm gathered safely in."

Are the lines a prayer? A plea? A petition? These are words you speak when the world is about to end.

Chief among Cohen's books of the strange is his formidable novel *Beautiful Losers*. With its intermingling of poetry and pornography, the sacred and the profane, it must have seemed a very strange book when published in 1966. It seems no less strange now.

As strange as Hubert Aquin's *Prochain Episode* in its politics, as strange as André Breton's *Nadja* in its pursuit of the feminine, Cohen's novel manages to seep love through the cracks of mockery and surrealism. Everything is a game in the novel, everything can be mocked, and yet the love and the prayers feel real even when mocked. The Book of Strange is also the Book of Longing and the Book of Prayer.

Leonard Cohen's narrator begins his bizarre confession with questions to a native historical figure of the 17th century recently re-envisioned by biographer-historian Allan Greer in *Mohawk Saint: Catherine Tekakwitha and the Jesuits*. "Catherine Tekakwitha, who are you?" And then, "Can I love you in my own way?" Famous for her quest for sacred knowledge and mystical – even ecstatic – experience, Tekakwitha was the leader of a group of Mohawk women who converted to Catholicism and according to Greer's account "renounced sex and marriage, while disciplining their bodies with fasting, flagellation, and deliberate exposure to the pain of fire and the discomfort of cold".

The narrator, an authority on a little-known aboriginal tribe, professes his desire to rescue Tekakwitha from the Jesuits and those who would claim to know her or own her. She was (one is tempted to say is) a magical person for Cohen and the most thoroughly-documented indigenous person of the Americas in the colonial period. Beatified by Pope John Paul II in 1980, and associated with ecology and virginity, she is officially the "Blessed Catherine Tekakwitha" now awaiting canonization. Early in the novel, the narrator's wife, Edith, cries out to Tekakwitha: "Help me, Saint Kateri!"

Constipated and alone in a treehouse, the narrator summons the dead Catherine in a mode of address that poet Eli Mandel characterizes as "clown-saint-word-magic language." There are four main characters in the novel, three of whom are dead: a politician-philosopher F., a narrator, his Indian wife Edith, and the Mohawk mystic, Catherine Tekakwitha. Critic George Woodcock refers to the characters as moving "in memory within a pattern". The pattern seems to be "a murderously ambiguous seduction/repulsion pattern" where the narrator idealizes Tekakwitha and then mocks his idealization; he raises her up in order to knock her down.

The declared purpose of the novel is to unveil a virgin, to shatter an icon, but Catherine Tekakwitha remains intact, elusive and unbroken.

"What is a saint?" the narrator asks and answers: "A saint is someone who has achieved a remote human possibility. It is impossible to say what the possibility is. I think it has something to do with the energy of love." Catherine Tekakwitha, who died at age 24 in Kahnawake, Quebec on April 17th, 1680, achieves, much like Simone Weil in our time, "a remote human possibility" and expresses "the energy of love". Her achievement is built on a life of prayer and service to others, severe discipline, sacrificial virginity and self-administered pain. The deprivation of herself and her community is so severe that F., in his long letter in Book Two of Cohen's novel, remarks: "O God, forgive me, but I see it on my thumb, the whole wintry village looks like a Nazi medical experiment."

One of the challenges of reading the novel is to determine at any given moment what voice it is written in. The central voice in the book – brisk and boisterous for a death-haunted, God-haunted narrative – praises, ridicules, idealizes, mocks, blasphemes and reveres, often in the same breath.

The novel says as much about its readers as any reader is likely to say about it. You can read the novel politically, sexually, mythically; you can read it as metafiction, as hallucination; you can read it as a late *Beat* work. The novel's characters are Beat in Jack Kerouac's sense of the word's associations with beatific and beaten; they lose beautifully.

You can read the novel theologically. The quest in *Beautiful Losers* is for God (or the Goddess), and for magic and mystery. Are magic and mystery still, in Cohen's word, afoot? The tentative conclusion F. draws is that they are afoot because of "the New Jew", "the founder of Magic Canada, Magic French Quebec, and Magic America".

"Every generation," says F., "must thank its Jews ... And its Indians."

Beautiful Losers is a political novel (you get a keen sense of the politics of grievance in Quebec), a homosexual novel (aside from the narrator's necrophilic relationship with a dead Indian, the main love bond is between F. and the unnamed narrator), a pornographic novel (it seems at times stuck in the oral and anal stages of Freud's development grid). And it is a book of drunken poetry and heart-piercing prayer, with almost as many prayers as Cohen's *Book of Mercy*.

Along with passages you'd want to frame or recite in a storm, there are pages of self-indulgent twaddle. Sometimes you find yourself agreeing with Stephen Scobie that *Beautiful Losers* "is the craziest Canadian novel ever written, the most beautiful, the most obscene, the most irrational." Sometimes you're happier with George Woodcock's assessment that it is tedious. "The burlesque element is overdone; the pop art use of comic strips and junky advertisements ... scenes of ... mechanical sexual stimulation follow each other in a diminuendo of effectiveness." Most of the time, I rest comfortably with Cohen's own evaluation: "*Beautiful Losers* is a love story, a psalm ... a satire, a prayer ... a disagreeable religious epic of incomparable beauty." The novel, haloed and hallucinogenic, is the sort of book for which the word phantasmagorical seems specifically invented. As much graphic novel and comic book as traditional narrative, it changes voice as frequently as *Sin City* changes scenes and storylines.

As readers, we are unaccustomed to having our sacred stones juggled so recklessly. We are not used to rapid transport from play to prayer, from brothel to prayer-house. As F. proclaims, "Games are nature's most beautiful creation. All animals play games, and the truly Messianic vision of the brotherhood of creatures must be based on the idea of the game." In *Beautiful Losers,* no line separates the sacred from the secular. The House of Play is also the House of Prayer.

In words transcribed from radio interviews with Eli Mandel and Phyllis Webb, Cohen says: "I was writing a liturgy ... a great mad confessional prayer." Is Catherine his mother-confessor? Lines attributed to his grandfather in "Lines From My Grandfather's Journal" seem comfortable in his own mouth: "It is strange that even now prayer is my natural language."

The prayers in *Beautiful Losers* range from the long Catherine-inspired dance-prayer of "God is alive. Magic is afoot", brought beautifully to song by Buffy Sainte-Marie, to short invocations of presence and mystery. The narrator asks, "Is All the World a Prayer?" The answer seems to be yes. Catherine prays, "O God, show me that the Ceremony belongs to Thee. Reveal to your servant a fissure in the Ritual. Change Thy World with the jawbone of a broken Idea. O my Lord, play with me."

Leonard Cohen's life's work excels in strangeness, whether it's spoofing the holy, mocking society and the self, or mixing the sophomoric with the sacramental. Like fellow-Montrealer Mordecai Richler, he seldom leaves a sacred cow unslaughtered or a platitude unskewered in his ironic poses. On the stage, in bearing and manners, he's the epitome of an aristocratic

Englishman, gracious and elegant; on the page he can be abrasive and unsparing in one breath, and tender and loving in another.

Stranger Music, an apt title for the most generous portion of his songs and poems currently on the market, encapsulates his lifelong signature. Cohen has put his life on the page, from the narcissistic youth slightly drunk on his own precocious talent, to the middle-aged singer and celebrity of madness and love, to the old man with self-deprecating humour and the wisdom of Ecclesiastes.

Clown. Rabbi. Mr. Cohen is a Blakean character who unifies opposites within himself: self-indulgence and discipline, narcissism and humility, lust and longing. He doesn't so much compare mythologies as he enfleshes them. Nothing human is alien to his wide-embracing heart as he insists on striking all the human notes: the banal, the satiric, the devout, the political, the sexual, the lyrical.

In his poem "The Genius", somewhat reminiscent of Philip Roth's conviction in *Operation Shylock* that within every Jew is a "mob of Jews", he can imaginatively project "a ghetto jew", "an apostate jew", "a banker jew", "a Broadway jew", "a doctor jew" and "a Dachau jew". In his work he's a scholar-Jew (*Beautiful Losers* entails a close reading of Catholic texts by priests who knew and worked with Tekakwitha and the clan-mothers) and a translating-Jew (think of his acknowledged debt to the Spanish poet Federico García Lorca in "Take this Waltz" and to the Greek poet Cavafy in "Alexandra Leaving", and his unacknowledged debt to Lorca again in "Dance Me to the End of Love"), as well as a remembering-Jew in his recreations of his grandfather's journals in "Lines From My Grandfather's Journal", where "The real deserts are outside of tradition". In the same poem he startles with an insight – "Prayer makes speech a ceremony" – and makes a vow: "Let me never speak casually."

A man with courtly manners and a scatalogical imagination, eloquent and shy, self-effacing and proud, Cohen arguably took the Canadian novel as far as it could go and stopped. He also took the Canadian lyric as far as it could go and stopped. And for the last forty-plus years he has devoted himself to song with a gravelly cigarette-and-wine voice. He's "the little Jew/ who wrote the Bible" and he's the novice under a Zen monk's care, and he's the Montrealer who deeply imbibed the fumes from Catholic incense.

"We who belong to this city have never left The Church. The Jews are in The Church as they are in the snow ... Every style in Montreal is the style of The Church." Cohen pens these words in his brief prose poem "Montreal". Not surprisingly, *Beautiful Losers* and many of his songs from "Suzanne" to "Joan of Arc" and "Song of Bernadette" make use of Catholic symbols.

Cohen has a statue of Catherine Tekakwitha on the stove of his house in Montreal. "She is one of my household spirits. I think she embodied in her own life, in her choices, many of the complex things that face us always. She spoke to me. She still speaks to me." What, one may ask, is a Jew, the grandson of rabbinical scholars, a member of his synagogue who lights candles on Friday night, doing with a saint in his house?

Leonard Cohen is a strange Jew by anyone's measure, one even liberal rabbis have difficulty with for his being a kind of real-life Pi from Yann Martel's novel, someone who has internalized Catholic symbols and Zen practice into his life and work, someone who grafts rather than excises. Cohen is nothing if not self-aware and he anticipates the critics:

> Anyone who says
> I'm not a Jew
> is not a Jew
> I'm very sorry
> but this decision
> is final

Be open, his life and words seem to say. Be open to the jazz and surrealism of things. As Lorca was, as Cohen is. Be full of prayer and play. Be a holy fool. Risk foolishness for spiritual growth and vulnerability for love. Gamble.

Open to ceremony and ritual, Cohen works within the constraints of form, often adhering to the traditions of metre and rhyme. Writing for Cohen is a ceremonial craft, a sacramental craft. You need to dress up for it, put on your best clothes, discipline your wayward and wanton mind and submit to discipline while paying attention to the whole.

Cohen has been a soundtrack for many Canadian lives; the man with "the golden voice" has crooned and rasped his way into the collective Canadian heart. And, if the Canadian Songwriters' Hall of Fame can induct five of his songs – "Suzanne", "Ain't No Cure For Love", "Bird on the Wire", "Everybody Knows", "Hallelujah" – many of us can quickly think of another five songs equally deserving.

"Suzanne", hauntingly beautiful, piercingly holy, is one of the great poem-songs of our time. Beauty and holiness abide in every breath. The song was constructed by an act of the imagination but it also touches on real experiences. Cohen looked out from the observation tower of the Notre-Dame-de-Bon-Secours chapel in the Montreal harbour to the Our Lady of the Harbour statue that stands with outstretched arms towards the St. Lawrence River. There was a real Suzanne, the wife of sculptor Armand Vaillancourt, who invited him to her home near the river where they shared a cup of tea. "The chord pattern was developed before a woman's name entered the song," Cohen remembers.

My own personal favourites, in addition to "Suzanne" and "Hallelujah", are "Who By Fire", "The Guests" and "If It Be Your Will". Just as I record this list I feel a pang of discomfort for my negligence – what about "Sisters of Mercy" with these gorgeous lines: "If your life is a leaf/ that the seasons tear off and condemn/ they will bind you with love/ that is graceful and green as a stem."

If there were a Canadian Poetry Hall of Fame, "I Have Not Lingered in European Monasteries", "Days of Kindness", "Roshi", "Go By Brooks", "Dance Me to the End of Love" and "Take This Waltz" would all belong in it, along with other poems from the best love lyrics in Canadian poetry.

For shaped and energized language, it's also hard to beat "Magic is Alive" from *Beautiful Losers* as an all-purpose utterance – a song, a poem, a prayer, a piece of prose, a prose poem. For me it is the single most powerful page in Canadian writing, ending in these dramatic words: "… and mind itself is Magic coursing through the flesh, and flesh itself is Magic dancing on a clock, and time itself the Magic Length of G-d."

Leonard Cohen's songs, even without the musical accompaniment, as poems on the page, stand up as among his most powerful utterances. You could write a book on his lines "There is a crack in everything./ That's how the light gets in" from "Anthem" in his CD *The Future*. Likewise for "There's a blaze of light in every word …" from the song "Hallelujah".

Cohen is someone with whom many make connections and identifications, whether his battle with depression or his steadfast journeying on a spiritual path.

He ripples gently through my life. On my first day on the job teaching literature at Mohawk College, my friend Wayne Allan walked into my cubicle and paraphrased a Cohen line: *I'm looking for a card so high and so wild I'll never have to deal another.* I thought to myself: *Isn't this an interesting place to work? Literature lives here.*

Cohen's life has vicariously shadowed mine. At my sister-in-law's wedding I read lines from "As the Mist Leaves No Scar"; I used lines from Cohen's "All There Is to Know about Adolph Eichmann" poem (he stresses the ordinariness of evil in reminding readers that Eichmann had ten fingers and ten toes) in my talk on Thomas Merton in Vancouver; Cohen's image of the kite in "The Kite is a Victim" inspired me to write a poem about my relationship with my son; I wrote an article for the *Literary Review of Canada* connecting *Beautiful Losers* to Allan Greer's *Mohawk Saint: Catherine Tekakwitha and the Jesuits*.

My wife and I own all the books, all the CDs; she sometimes arranges birthday parties "for Lenny" with a cloth spread over the living room carpet and wine and cheese brought in from the kitchen.

We have a photograph of the man in our bedroom, we've gone to two of his Toronto concerts, we play "The Guests" at late-night parties and "Closing Time" if the guests still don't get the hint that it's time to go. Once we even tried to drink his wine.

I had heard on the CBC that Cohen's favourite wine after a concert was Château Latour. He made a point of saying that it was reasonably priced. I went to the LCBO and asked for a case.

Suffice to say, a single bottle cost more than I would generally pay for a case of my usual tipple.

I continue to make notes on his work, most recently on his last published book, *Book of Longing*.

> *reading leonard cohen's book of longing. flyweight. but something winsome and winning about it. homemade. it has a homemade quality, handmade. heartmade. one man's doodles, images and words. one man's memories, including one with the then Prime Minister, Pierre Trudeau: "He was kind and powerful. He asked me to read him a poem. And then he asked me for another. And another ..." you read the book and say to yourself: now i know why a lot of women like this man. something disarmingly boyish about him. women want to mother him or sleep with him.*
>
> *cohen has a high degree of honesty. that appeals, too. he lets all the moods and desires that inhabit his being out. he gives them all a voice. he has a wide range of voices.*
>
> *the metre and rhyme that usually work for him in this book don't. they usually make for ceremony and ritual. in this book they're tired and worn techniques. lifeless.*
>
> *still for all that there's something appealing about the book. cohen says here i am. i'm old, i have memories, a few debts to pay, still have some playfulness in me, some prayer. he has a lot of g--d references. he's not afraid of failure, not afraid of falling on his face and making an ass of himself. some of the poems seem self-amusement exercises at least as much as they're publishable poems.*

a very human book. maybe his warmest, most foolish, most self-indulgent, most humble, most spiritual. simple words from a complex man.

"I don't have much to give you, but I'll give you everything I've got." That's how Leonard Cohen begins his concerts now, with truth and a lie. The lie is that he doesn't have much to give; the truth is that he really does give you everything he has.

He steps on stage with his band, they launch into their first number and they keep playing until intermission and then he and they come out again and play until closing time. There's no warm-up band, there's no other performer. It's the man and his gifted musicians and backup singers for three hours of art and entertainment. At the end of the evening he thanks the audience for its gracious attention to his neurosis and alchemy.

If you're lucky, you may get to hear "Boogie Street" and these lines:

> So come, my friends, be not afraid.
> We are so lightly here.
> It is in love that we are made;
> In love we disappear.

The lines have had resonance for me. I was able to write my own little tribute-poem based on them. I entitled it "lightly here".

> we're all lightly here, says the tao and
> the zen, says the bible, says leonard

cohen in a song, we're all so lightly
here ... our roots an inch or two,
our time a blink or two ...
what are you going to do ... paint a
picture, scratch a word, sing a song ...
when danger approaches, an arab proverb
says sing to it ... when oblivion comes,
sing to it.

In our bedroom photo of Leonard Cohen, he's seated on a slab of stone, a stone wall behind him and a granite-like tree. The sun is on his face, his eyes are shut, he's wearing a monk's robe, with his hands in a meditative gesture, body in the lotus position, his hair short-cropped the way monks' hair often is. He looks serene, he looks grounded, deeply *here*.

VII Harold Bloom's Jesus

When you meet Jesus of Nazareth in the pages of the New Testament, the encounter is often electric and transformative. When Saul Bellow writes to Stephen Mitchell after his reading of Mitchell's *The Gospel According to Jesus: a New Translation and guide to His Essential Teachings for Believers and Unbelievers,* Bellow confesses: "Jesus overwhelmed me ... I was moved when I read Gospels ... I was moved out of myself by Jesus ... Jesus moved me beyond all bounds by his deeds and his words." In a short essay on Jesus with the subtitle "On Tolerance and Christianity", the Australian critic Clive James concludes with this sentence: "The bird of morning will never sing all night long, but nor, if we are wise, will the memory of that man ever die." Jesus moves people, opens hearts and minds, sparks new beginnings.

Harold Bloom's encounter with Jesus is less emotional than Bellow's, less dramatic than that of James, more intellectual, more academic, more distantly removed from the central concerns of his heart, but no less interesting. He reads Jesus as a fellow Jew, a dangerous and charismatic ancestor because, in the assessment of Cynthia Ozick, "Within the bowels of the Bloomian structure there lives, below all, the religious imagination: sibylline, vatic, divinatory ..." and his work constitutes "a long Theophanous prose-poem, a rationalized version of Blake's heroic Prophetic Books."

Bloom is a large literary figure, "a colossus among critics", with the insatiable appetite of his favourite Shakespearean character Falstaff. He holds up the balanced sentences and judgments of Dr. Johnson as his critical model, but his own writing has more in common with the ironic and aphoristic Oscar Wilde. He is what he has read, and he has read prodigiously. Fittingly the subtitle of his most recent book, *The Anatomy of Influence,* is *Literature as a Way of Life.* He has lived the literary life.

In his early scholastic years Bloom read for the small, essential detail, as in his commentary on individual poems of William Blake in a volume of Blake's poetry and prose edited by David V. Erdman in 1965. In recent years, he has read for the large, and has engaged with many of the world's grand visions and imaginative constructs. He swashbucklingly romps across time, meaning and memory, across Blake and Shakespeare, across Whitman, Emerson and Stevens, with little to say about specific words and lines. He buries traces of his expansive reading in his public-seeking voice. Why encumber the general reading public with indexes, bibliographies and footnotes when you're dispensing wisdom?

In *Jesus and Yahweh,* he passingly alludes – without footnotes or commentaries – to prominent New Testament scholars from E.P. Sanders and J.P. Meier to Wayne A. Weeks, Jaroslav Pelikan and Donald Harman Akenson. Along with a handful of acknowledged books, there are hundreds of unacknowledged books behind this one volume of Bloomian critical religious thought. He still reads for details, but subsumes them in the architectural grandeur of his writing. In sheer quantity of books devoured, he seems to have outread anyone currently living. Only the dead Northrop Frye, were he to rise, would be a worthy competitor.

David Markson cracks a joke in his novel called *This is Not a Novel:*

Did Professor Bloom take any books with him, do you know?

Someone said he had a twenty-six-volume complete Joseph Conrad. It's only a weekend cruise.

If Bloom were the man in Clemens Kalischer's photograph of an anonymous Jew reading by the window, books would engulf the room, conceal the window, and spread like ivy over the bench and chair. In his hand would be his central ball of light, *The Complete Works of William Shakespeare;* on his lap would be William Blake, the poet who led him as a boy from his first language, Yiddish, to his second, English; and by his side would sit Walt Whitman, Ralph Waldo Emerson and Wallace Stevens. With a face at once mischievous and sad, he has of late been writing more religious criticism than literary criticism. His reputation may finally rest more on his interpretations of religions and religious texts than on literature and literary texts, although, to be fair to Bloom, he does not usually distinguish the religious from the literary. Yahweh and Jesus to Bloom are literary characters. Religion to Bloom, following Stevens, is a kind of poetry – poetry for the masses – although not the supreme poetry, since that place is occupied by Shakespeare.

Religious texts and the personalities found therein are literary constructs and literary figures. Bloom himself slips into literature. Once you've seen a picture of his hound-dog face you can't read Joyce's Leopold Bloom in *Ulysses* without seeing his bedraggled Yale University descendant. Bloom is boisterously logocentric and bibliocentric; he may or may not have an appetite like his literary ancestor for drink and women, but he certainly shares Leopold's infatuation with language. He is a Seussian geyser of gab.

Even more than Alberto Manguel, man-at-read is Harold Bloom reading. Whatever holiness, whatever magic, whatever salvation Bloom believes in, his belief resides in the holiness, in the magic and in the salvific quality of the book. If "you are to grow in self-knowledge, become more introspective, discover the authentic treasures of insight and of compassion and of spiritual discernment and of a deep bond to other solitary individuals", you have no choice but to turn to the book. The book for Bloom primarily means story and poetry books, imaginative literature, which he argues, in varying degrees, comprises the scriptures of Judaism, Christianity and Islam.

Ever pugilistic and hyperbolic, Bloom thinks in aphorisms rather than in sustained argument, much like his early critical master Northrop Frye. (The pugilist is what Edward Said most admires in Bloom: "Bloom's work is centered around struggle, and very restricted notions of power, domination, and repression ... One doesn't just write: one writes against, or in opposition to, or in some dialectical relationship with other writers and writing ...".) He is also an elegist mourning the loss of reading and deep reflection and the defeat of cognitively and aesthetically superior texts (the Hebrew Bible) by cognitively and aesthetically inferior ones (the Christian Bible). How, Bloom challenges, can an astute reader prefer one story (that of Jesus) to the many in the Hebrew Bible? He regards the Hebrew Bible, or what Christians call the Old Testament, as being composed principally of narrative, of story, whereas the New Testament provides revisionist commentary.

Nevertheless, Bloom regards Jesus as the largest figure in Jewish history. (Freud plays second fiddle.) "Whether in aphorism or in parable, Jesus speaks in riddles. He is the poet of the riddle, anticipating Dante, Shakespeare, Cervantes, John Donne, and even Lewis Carroll and James Joyce, as well as Kierkegaard, Emerson, Nietzsche, Kafka, and many others in the literary and spiritual tradition of the West." So says Harold Bloom in one sweeping breath in *Jesus and Yahweh*, characteristically oblivious to hesitation or qualification. Bloom says other provocative and insightful things about Jesus in the same volume:

All Western irony is a repetition of Jesus' enigmas/riddles, in amalgam with the ironies of Socrates.

Jesus is the Jewish Socrates, and surpasses Plato's mentor as the supreme master of dark wisdom.

Bloom tends to emphasize the words of Jesus over his deeds, his literary presence rather than his spiritual presence, although Bloom is clearly aware of Jesus' solidarity with the poor and disenfranchised.

The American Jesus may become too compromised by the Christian Right to go on as the intimate friend of the dispossessed.

One pauses to ponder the ramifications of this statement, given that one of the United States' biggest exports, along with movies, is the American Jesus, who for a long time now has been refashioned by the frightened and panic-filled voice of the Right, with its adherents militaristically promoting the Rapture throughout the globe.

At most, one tries to write a footnote to the endlessly rich and fruitful life of Jesus. The peasant Jew from Nazareth wrote only once in sand and yet he has probably spawned more books, more libraries, than any other person on earth. Thankfully the Dr. Kings and the Dorothy Days and countless nameless ones are still, in His name, at work in the world. His variegated face, along with the Buddha's, shines across the world.

Harold Bloom has been slouching towards Nazareth for some time now. The watershed work is The Charles Eliot Norton Lectures published as *Ruin the Sacred Truths: Poetry and Belief from the Bible to the Present* (1989) in which he argues that imaginative literature resists "the categories of sacred and secular". You can say, declares Bloom, that all high literature is secular or that all strong poetry is sacred, but you can't say that one piece of art is more sacred or more secular than another. *Ruin,* a title pinched from Andrew Marvell, marks the beginning of Bloom's abandonment of Hebrew and Greek terminologies for the literary priesthood as his principal mode of address, and his adoption of plain English pitched at as broad an audience as possible.

Bloom may not have originated the phrase "The American Religion" but he has stamped it with his own formidable personality. The American Religion – built around the indigenous faiths of the Mormons, the Southern Baptists, the Pentecostals and so on – sees God as an extension of the self, as a being in direct and intimate relationship with the self. Americans have a very personal Jesus, a personal Lord and Saviour. "The American Religion," says Bloom, "is neither a Christian 'believing that' nor a Judaic 'trusting in'; it is knowing ..." (Elsewhere Bloom pronounces: Christians believe; Jews trust; Muslims surrender.)

This very personal Jesus whose principal concerns seem to be abortion and gays is usually wrapped in the American flag as if he were born somewhere in the hills of Kentucky. He is invited into one's heart, often in an assembly with all the enthusiasm of a winning American basketball team. Once he takes up residence there, one no longer needs to question or struggle or study; all of one's needs are met; one knows. The important thing seems to be not so much that Americans love Jesus as it is Jesus loves Americans; he has given them the divine mission of bringing light to the world's darkness – not infrequently in the shock and awe of gunfire and bombs. America exports this faith successfully to Asia, Africa and Latin America, along with Hollywood movies, flush toilets and weaponry. Bloom wryly adds: "A religion of the self is not likely to be a religion of peace, since the American self tends to define itself through its war against otherness. If your knowing ultimately tells you that you are beyond nature, having long preceded it, then your natural acts cannot sully you." This religion seems to have little connection to the Jesus of the Gospels, where the stranger is lifted up and service to others is the highest good.

Bloom's Jesus is a sayer of dark things, a Trickster, a poet, a Gnostic, a Pharisee, a kind of contrarian, a master of parable, riddle and aphorism. Bloom draws his water from the wells of the Gospels of Thomas and Mark. He has little appreciation of, and not much patience for, Matthew, Luke, John and Saints Peter and Paul. He sees Jesus as a first-century Jewish Hamlet, an enigma who trucks in enigmas. According to Bloom, there are "at least seven Jesuses in the New Covenant", eight if you include the American Jesus. Such a figure is close to universality, says Bloom, but "… his thousand guises are too bewildering for coherence." Jesus can shape-shift quicker than Proteus; he's an abyss whose face resembles the gazer. Not surprisingly, Bloom's Jesus looks very much like Bloom himself.

Bloom seems deaf to the power of the parables and the strength – artistic and spiritual – of Paul's letters. Jesus, says Bloom, principally teaches awareness and perception, not love. His Jesus lives comfortably with ambiguity and contradiction, with gaps. Bloom also seems puzzlingly blind to biblical narrative techniques in both the Hebrew and Christian Bibles. They suggest more than they say. One needs to enter the narratives in the spirit of Bloom's hero Emerson and read creatively, helping to construct the final impression of the prose.

The Jesus from which I draw strength includes the Parables, the Lord's Prayer, the Beatitudes, the Sermon on the Mount. This Jesus embraces children, stands in solidarity with the poor and the oppressed, makes loving connections to women, washes his friends' feet, and shares food and wine with friends and strangers alike. This Jesus curses hypocrites, overturns the money-changers' tables, and commissions us to feed the hungry, clothe the naked, comfort the sick and the grieving and visit the imprisoned. He is found in the incomplete and fragmented scrolls of the early record keepers of his life and work, but also in the subsequent embroideries. As poet-priest Gerard Manley Hopkins wrote so memorably over a hundred years ago, "... Christ plays in ten thousand places ..."

I hear Jesus in the music of Bach, in the words of Simone Weil and the liberation theology of Ernesto Cardenal, in the Japanese novelist and biographer Shusaku Endo's *Life of Jesus*. I see him in Henri Matisse's stained glass in the chapel at Vence, in Marc Chagall's crucifixion paintings, in Pier Paolo Pasolini's *The Gospel According to St. Matthew* and Denys Arcand's *Jesus of Montreal*, in Russian icons, in African paintings of the black Christ. I celebrate the Jewish Jesus and the cosmic Christ, the Jesus of Nazareth and of Hamilton, the wine-drinker, the storyteller and the embracer of strangers.

What Bloom seems immune to is any appreciation of the two thousand years of embroideries that have stitched themselves into the original garment. He praises the New Testament's words but ignores the accumulated Christ-inspired embroideries over the centuries – the liturgies, the ceremonies, the rituals, the exegeses, the artworks, the prayers, the attempts to re-enact a life of generosity and forgiveness. The omissions seem odd for a man of Bloom's breadth. His Hamlet, it seems to me, would not only include Hamlet as he appears in the original Quarto and Folio versions, but also Hamlet in the words of the great critics, himself included, and the stage and film performances in our day from Lawrence Olivier and Richard Burton to Mel Gibson and Ethan Hawke. All – texts, commentaries and re-projections – are part of a common tradition. Bloom's Jesus is an adept word-magician, a subtle hair-splitter, an argumentative iconoclast – again, a bit like Bloom himself – but ultimately alone and godforsaken.

There is a fullness to Jesus, a largeness, even given the incomplete and sometimes contradictory fragments in the New Testament and in the Gnostic Gospels. There is a Zen Jesus (to which Vietnamese poet-monk Thich Nhat Hanh has contributed in his *Living Christ, Living Buddha*), a First Nations Jesus (who has spoken more personally and plainly on nature?), a radical and even revolutionary Jesus in his turning upside down of the world's values (consider Bob Dylan's "The Times They Are A-Changin'" or Johnny Cash's "Man In Black"). This many-sided Jesus comes out of Jewish traditions, which he periodically critiques and frequently augments, but he is not confined to his roots or even to his people.

The Son of Man crucified continues to be a universal emblem of human suffering, just as the bemused Buddha represents a universal emblem of human inscrutability in the face of suffering. Bloom being a word man rather than an image man – unlike Alberto Manguel, for instance, who is both – has nothing to say about these powerful images. He is speechless before the two great projections of the human face: the image of the anguished face and contorted body, like something out of Francis Bacon, and the image of the enchanting smile, reminiscent of the *Mona Lisa*. I will speak of the first image rather than the second even though I have enormous respect for the second image and agree with the poet-monk Thich Nhat Hanh, that the living Christ and the living Buddha share a great deal of common ground.

Has Bloom forgotten how African-Americans have historically appropriated the Jewish story in the Bible as their own story? Is it such a stretch that struggling peoples from southeast Asia to Africa to Latin America would internalize the story of a crucified Jew as their own story? Is Bloom not familiar with the beautiful ingesting of the story of Jesus, through art and word, by farmers and fishermen on the islands of Solentiname in Lake Nicaragua? Edited by Philip and Sally Scharper and presented by Ernesto Cardenal, the book is called *The Gospel in Art by the Peasants of Solentiname*.

Jesus has a presence in the world far beyond what the United States has done to his name or image. Where pain is, where suffering is, Jesus is.

Where Bloom is strongest is in his clear and convincing reclamation of Jesus as a Jew for Jews. Jesus needs to be seen in his Jewish roots before he can be transplanted to other places and climes. His Jewishness should be a given, and widely understood. But even as enlightened a Pope as John Paul II regarded

Christianity and Judaism as sister religions rather than recognizing Judaism as the mother religion. (I say this knowing that Bloom follows the Protestant theologian Donald Harman Akenson, to whom he dedicates his *Jesus and Yahweh,* in awareness of a mixed and complicated parentage: "Donald Akenson emphasizes the paradox that Christianity was invented in the first century C.E., before Rabbinical Judaism developed in the second century: Paul precedes Akiba.")

Many seem to forget that Jesus went to synagogue, not to church; he observed Jewish feasts and holy days; he was conversant with Jewish scripture; he taught by means of a Jewish art form – the parable. Too often, as with Simone Weil, the Jewishness of Jesus is ignored or downplayed as if Jesus were born a gentile or founded a new Christian religion distinct from its parent. The founding of a Christ-centred religion most scholars would attribute to the organizational genius of another Jew, Paul of Tarsus – or in Akenson's nomenclature, "Saint Saul".

For me, Bloom does great service to Jesus by rescuing him from the Christian box where priests and pastors have safely and conveniently kept him, and for too long have monopolized the conversation around him. My own conviction is that the Jewish Jesus, as opposed to the American Jesus, is far more radical, and troublesome, than what many churches would be comfortable with.

When I look around my own personal library, I see that Bloom has company in his reclamation of a fellow Jew. I see Irving Layton's *For My Brother Jesus* (1976) – "O crucified poet/ your agonized face haunts me ..." – on the third shelf of my poetry section. Leonard Cohen's song "Suzanne" (1966) – "And Jesus was a sailor/ When he walked upon the water/ And he spent a long time watching/ From his lonely wooden tower ..." – still rumbles in my head. Gila Safran Naveh's *Biblical Parables and*

Their Modern Re-creations (2000) gives Jesus the central place as the supreme parable-speaker of the Jewish parabolic tradition and, in a certain sense, the father of Kafka, Calvino and Borges. There are also Joseph Brodsky's Nativity poems, which I gave to a friend, Hannah Arendt's thoughts on nativity and the Nativity in *The Human Condition* (1958) –"It is this faith in and hope for the world that found perhaps its most glorious and most succinct expression in the few words the Gospels announced their 'glad tidings': 'A child has been born unto us;'" – and that strange Jewish scholar Geza Vermes, who converted to Catholicism and then reconverted to Judaism and says in *The Authentic Gospel of Jesus* (2003): "The historical Jesus, a religious genius who lived, taught and died in Jewish Palestine in the first century of the time reckoning named after him, has been at the centre of my scholarly preoccupation since the late 1960s." These are a few of the Jewish volumes in my library that predate Bloom's proclamation of the Jewishness of Jesus.

Gentile scholars, too, have worked hard to reposition Jesus in his Jewish context. One thinks of Dominic Crossan's *The Historical Jesus: The Life of a Mediterranean Jewish Peasant* (1991), John. Meier's *A Marginal Jew: Rethinking the Historical Jesus*, two volumes so far (1991 & 1994), which Bloom quotes in *Jesus and Yahweh,* and the Protestant scholar E.P. Sanders' *Jesus and Judaism* (1985), similarly referenced. Three recent works, Bruce Chilton's *Rabbi Jesus* (2000), Rex Weyler's *The Jesus Sayings: The Quest for His Authentic Message* (2008) and Barrie A. Wilson's *How Jesus Became Christian* (2008) also make the case for the Jewishness of Jesus. The Bibles – Hebrew and Christian – are, after all, collections of books written by Jews about Jews. Leonard Cohen rightly says within playful poetic licence: "I'm the little Jew who wrote the Bible." All of it: Paul's letters as much as Ecclesiastes' wisdom.

Bloom has no patience for the Judaic-Christian tradition. In *Jesus and Yahweh* he writes, "I am dubious about the phrase 'the Jewish-Christian tradition.' Now it refers to a particular sociopolitical phenomenon, and seems part of the alliance between the United States and Israel." Is this Harold Bloom or Edward Said speaking?

Bloom sees Jesus within the context of Judaism, but Christianity as an altogether different phenomenon.

In the *Battle of the Books* – interesting that Bloom would see the conflict between Judaism and Christianity almost exclusively in terms of texts – Bloom must ruefully accept that the New usurps the Old. "The central procedure of the New Testament is the conversion of the Hebrew Bible into the Old Testament," Bloom scolds. The Hebrew Bible or the Tanakh is rearranged so that it ends with Malachi and not with II Chronicles. And the New Testament "is designed as a prism through which its precursor text is to be read, revised, and interpreted". Paul, claims Bloom, "is particularly adept at this reworking, but all who came after him ... are superbly gifted in the arts of usurpation, reversal, and appropriation." The New Testament "is obsessed with its anxious relationship to the Law and the Prophets" and is "the strongest and most successful creative misreading in all of textual history".

The battle ends for Bloom when the masses read or hear, and accept as truth, the words, "Believe that Jesus was the Christ and you will be saved and live eternally." These words, argues Bloom, in their irresistible simplicity, invincible on the popular level, proved to be challenged, if at all, only by Islam's "Submit to Allah on the authority of Muhammed ... and you will be rewarded in the life to come." He oversimplifies. It seems to me that Paul's opening up the Jesus movement to gentiles, the power of the parables and the Sermon on the Mount, Jesus becoming a universal embodiment of love and forgiveness in the face of death and destruction, would also be contributing factors in the spread of the movement.

The *Battle of the Books,* in Swift's great phrase, is personal for Bloom. It brings to mind his relationship with his own father figure, Northrop Frye. Belatedly he tells Frye, "No text, secular or religious, fulfills another text, and all who insist otherwise merely homogenize literature." In opposition to Frye's tendency to read the Hebrew Bible as a precursor text which reaches its fulfillment and apotheosis in the Christian Bible, Bloom thunders back with that daring Protestant, Nietzsche: "Who is the interpreter and what power does he seek to gain over the text?"

Is no dialogue possible, then, between a mother and an aberrant child? "Can the New Testament be read as less polemically and destructively revisionary of the Hebrew Bible than it actually is?" "Not by me," Bloom responds to his own question.

The dialogue is perhaps more easily conducted by art, within art. Think of Marc Chagall's "White Crucifixion" (1938) where Jesus (Yeshua) wears a loincloth with two black stripes resembling the Jewish tallith, and at his feet is the seven-branched candlestick. A synagogue burns in the painting and Torah scrolls are torched. Some Jewish elders lament, others flee. Chagall's biographer, Franz Meyer, writes, "For Chagall, suffering remains man's lasting fate. It is not his divine but his human nature that Christ's suffering preserves."

Bloom has added an important and beautiful book to ongoing Jesus lore. He has engaged deeply with his Jewish brother, elucidating him, even at times being humbled by him.

My own view is that a broad public dialogue will not commence in honesty until Israel no longer needs the financial and political support of the sizable Christian Zionist constituency in the United States. Such dialogue is to be desired. The possibility of Judaism reincorporating one of its great sons into the family, as artists in image and word have already begun to do, and the possibility of Christianity loosening its monopoly on a Jewish gift to the world, would engender a new ecumenism for the future.

VIII The Last Jewish Intellectuals: Susan Sontag and Edward Said (or, Two New Yorkers Reading and Writing)

You wouldn't expect a novelist to write a story, a character sketch, about two essayists, even if she's a Nobel prizewinner and the essayists are famous wherever books are read. Such is the case, however, in Nadine Gordimer's "Dreaming about the Dead" from her short story collection *Beethoven Was One-Sixteenth Black and Other Stories*. Gordimer catches the conversational tics, the mannerisms, and the physicality of her two New York friends in a short piece of writing that is at once a eulogy and a celebration.

She calls Said, a former music critic for *The Nation*, to her table first, and remarks that he "never needed to prove his mental superiority by professional dowdiness and dandruff". He "never had to command" since "there is something in those eyes fathomless black with ancient Middle Eastern ancestry, that has no need of demanding words".

At a Chinese restaurant in what is presumably Manhattan, the narrator sits down at a table with Edward Said and awaits Susan Sontag, the English journalist Anthony Sampson, and an unnamed person who never arrives. Said and the narrator "plunge right away into our customary eager exchanges of interpretations of political events, international power-mongering, national religious and secular conflicts, the obsessional scaffolding of human existence ..." Sampson enters next; then Sontag.

Sontag: avidity incarnate. *More* is the operative word throughout her life: more books, more ideas, more art, more talk, more travel, more risk, more experiment, and above all, even when stricken with an incurable form of blood cancer, more life. "Always larger-than-life ... a mythical goddess, Athena-Medea statue with that magnificent head of black hair asserting this doubling authority, at once inspiring, menacing, unveiling a sculptor's bold marble features, gouged by commanding eyes." Said has "eyes fathomless dark" and Sontag "commanding eyes". They both have large selves with extensive wakes.

"Edward is a Palestinian, he's also in his ethics of human being, a Jew, we know that from his writings, his exposure of the orientalism within us, the invention of the Other ..." Sontag? "If Sontag's a Jew, she too, has identity beyond that label, hers has been one with Vietnamese, Sarajevans, many others, to make up the sum of self." (One of Sontag's acts of heroism was to fly in and out of Sarajevo during a time of gunfire and explosions to mount a multilingual production of *Waiting for Godot*. There is now a street in the city named after her.)

The narrator in Gordimer's story mixes the present moment with recollections of the past. "The Said apartment on the Upper West Side in New York had what you'd never expect to walk in on, two grand pianos taking up one of the livingrooms." Said tells the narrator that she has writing but that he has writing and music. "Edward. A composer. What he always was, should have been; but there was too much demand upon him from the threatening outer world?" Edward was a scholar, "a politico-philosophical intellect, an enquirer of international morality in the order of the world, a life whose driving motivation was not chosen but placed upon him: Palestinian". In Gordimer's dream-story, he's working on a symphony "based on Jewish folk songs and Palestinian laments or chants".

Gordimer's emphasis on Said's connection to music is not misplaced. Friend and conductor Daniel Barenboim, in a tribute to Said entitled "Sound and vision" (*The Guardian,* October 25, 2004) says this about music and Said: "The paradox consists of the fact that music is only sound, but sound, in itself, is not music. There lies Said's main idea as a musician who was also an excellent pianist." Barenboim suggests that Said's political ideas of interdependence and integration derived first from musical experience. "In music, there are no independent elements."

Critic and biographer Mustapha Marrouchi, in *Edward Said at the Limits,* also says something valuable about Said in relation to musical taste:

> *His inclination to composers of the late classical and early romantic school – Beethoven, Wagner, Strauss, (but not Mozart so much, because the levity and ease of composition that characterized Mozart's work clashed with Said's instinctive conviction that artistic creation had to be difficult, requiring an effort that could be painful and filled with self-doubt) – is strong, to say the least.*

In his last work, published posthumously – *On Late Style: Music and Literature Against the Grain* – Said writes about the difficult and discordant final works of Beethoven and others.

If music is at the heart of Edward Said, then words and books are at the heart of Susan Sontag. In The Nadine Gordimer Lecture, published as "At the Same Time: The Novelist and Moral Reasoning" in *At the Same Time: Essays and Speeches* and delivered in Cape Town months before her death, Sontag minimalistically utters these words: "Love words, agonize over sentences. And pay attention to the world." In the same book, she defines herself as principally a reader:

If literature has engaged me as a project, first as a reader and then as a writer, it is as an extension of my sympathies to other selves, other domains, other dreams, other words, other territories of concern.

In a late essay from *Where the Stress Falls*, she echoes Virginia Woolf's words: "Sometimes I think heaven must be one continuous unexhausted reading."

Gordimer in her charming story of resurrected friends goes quickly to the heart of Sontag's contribution to world letters: "… she shamed the complacent acceptance of suffering as no-one else has done. Since Goya!" I think that Gordimer's right about this. Sontag will last as the writer of a few important essays, but primarily as a chronicler of pain, the pain of others more than her own considerable pain. She helped change the diction around illness and pain, challenging militaristic metaphors on cancer, humanizing the discussion around AIDs, and finally, in a work of great compassion, extending her own pain-ridden self into the selves of other sufferers. In this way, she moved from the verbal equivalents of Frida Kahlo's personal self-portraits of a body on a rack, a body with a steel shaft down its chest, to something more like Marc Chagall's universal Christ-figures on a cross.

She could, however, be difficult. My friend B. W. Powe told me, after organizing the "Living Literacies" Conference at York University in November 2002, that Sontag was the most difficult and demanding person to deal with, stretching patience beyond the endurance necessary for George Steiner, Jean Baudrillard and Gayatri Chakravorty Spivak. She didn't show her tenderness. She kept it for her son in her novel *The Volcano Lover,* in one of the most beautiful dedications a mother ever wrote for a son: "**For David** beloved son, comrade." The use of the word comrade suggests a joint mission.

In Gordimer's short story, she gives advice, she issues commands, she controls the table. She tells Edward, for instance, to choose prawns over duck or chicken, as if he weren't capable of making the decision himself. Sontag's last words to her son David Rieff were, "I want to tell you ..." Ever the teacher, she extols the need for quality and excellence. See Ozu's films, read Barthes' essays, see Hodgkin's oils, and how can you possibly not be familiar with Simone Weil and John Berger?

Edward Said (1935-2003): professor of comparative literature at Columbia University, a writer in Arabic as well as English, culturally a Christian, a music critic, literary critic and theorist, a world-class piano player, activist, polemicist, memoirist, stone thrower. I remember the beginnings of an online *New York Times* obituary on Said the night of his death. The reviewer began with a reference to Said's having thrown a stone at an Israeli lookout post on the Lebanese border. As I recall, there was even a photograph of the stone-throwing. I was stunned. The stone had more prominence than what Said had done for literature and music, or for Palestine. I immediately fired off an angry email in protest. I suspect that hundreds of people that night did likewise. Thankfully, by the afternoon the morning's account of his life was fuller and more balanced, but still treated him as a kind of exotic foreigner, apparently oblivious to the fact that Said was above all else a New Yorker. He was a homeboy treated as a foreigner. *The Guardian*'s obituary, in contrast, was much warmer and more personal than the *Times*'.

I sometimes wonder if Said's model for a binational state in Israel-Palestine was a recasting of his vision of New York City:

> ... *most of the fruit and vegetable shops are Korean, the newsstands Indian or Pakistani, hot-dog carts and small luncheonettes Greek, street pedlars Senegalese; a large population of Dominicans, Haitians, Ecuadorans and Jamaicans have made inroads into proletarian domains once populated by Blacks and Puerto Ricans, just as Japanese, Chinese and Vietnamese children play the role once reserved for bright, upwardly-mobile and professionally inclined Eastern European Jews.*

New York as the world's marketplace. Israel-Palestine couldn't exactly be the world in the same way, but perhaps it could, in theory at least, house a range of religious and secular belief and expression similar to New York's smorgasbord of nationalities and ethnicities.

Susan Sontag (1933-2004): born Susan Lee Rosenblatt, more conversant in her early years with Roman Catholicism than with Judaism, the eternal student, ever the adorer and promoter of other artists' work, filmmaker, cultural critic, novelist, essayist, journal keeper, theatre director, New Yorker – whose body was taken to Paris for burial – Europeanist, francophile. She was treated as a homegirl in the *Times* obituary even though she had spent many years outside New York City. She had come a long way from her adolescence, when her largest dream was simply "to grow up and come to New York and write for *Partisan Review* and be read by 5,000 people".

In mid-to-late life she wanted to enter literature grandly as a novelist. She entered humbly instead as an essayist, more skilled in elucidating this world than conjuring and enfleshing imaginary worlds. In Hilary Mantel's comment in a *Los Angeles Times* book review, "What ultimately matters about Sontag ... is what she has defended: the life of the mind, and the necessity for reading and writing as 'a way of being fully human.'" To read and write was Sontag's particular way of being fully human.

Said and Sontag were New Yorkers, lovers of literature, "militant readers" (in Sontag's phrase), defenders of the underdog, victims of cancer after excruciating and heroic battles, people with gargantuan appetites. Neither wanted to sleep either for a short time or a long time. They were too afraid of missing something, or being unable to rethink or even rewrite something. Said's brief meditation on sleeplessness from the final page of his autobiographical memoir, *Out of Place,* seems to speak for himself and Susan Sontag:

> *For me, sleep is death, as is any diminishment in awareness ... Sleeplessness for me is a cherished state, to be desired at almost any cost; there is nothing for me as invigorating as the early-morning shedding of the shadowy half-consciousness of a night's loss, reacquainting myself with what I might have lost completely a few hours earlier. I occasionally experience myself as a cluster of flowing currents. I prefer this to the idea of a solid self ... These currents, like the themes of one's life, are borne along during the waking hours, and at their best require no reconciling, no harmonizing.*

Edward Said's mother also died of cancer; she had great difficulty sleeping. Perhaps Said's refusal to sleep, or his desire at least to sleep as little as possible, is part of his mother's legacy – or his defiance towards it.

David Schiff in *The Nation* (November 26, 2007) – the magazine for which Said wrote music criticism – recalls having had Sontag in the fall and Said in the spring as teachers in a core humanities course; the experience occurred in the early years of Said's teaching. Sontag would arrive a quarter-hour late for a 9:00 a.m. session, "bleary, bloodshot and seductively bohemian". She refused to teach Faust, characterizing it as a "pain in the ass", and preferred to show Tod Browning's 1932 cult classic *Freaks.* Said, with his tailor-made suits and his aristocratic bearing, insisted on "total devotion to the text", whether Shakespeare or Dostoyevsky. For all their differences, Schiff experienced a Sontag line coming to life from both teachers: "All my work says be serious, be passionate, wake up."

Said and Sontag jointly enfleshed another Sontag line: "Literature is the house of nuance and contrariness against the voice of simplification."

My first encounter with Sontag came through a photograph of her (young, shockingly beautiful with a wave of white mixed with her raven black hair) and my reading of "Against Interpretation". I think that I read the essay in a journal or anthology before I read the book of the same title. The essay was written in 1964. It stands up well. Given the amount of academic jargon heaped on works of art, it stands perhaps even more defiantly now than it did then. We are even further now from "an erotics of art" than we were then. I remember how hard the essay hit me at the time. Someone at last is telling the truth, I thought. The first important response to *Huckleberry Finn* is to laugh, and in subsequent readings, if the laughter is diminished then something is wrong with one's critical appraisal. Tears are the first appropriate response to *King Lear.* Great art goes straight into the bloodstream. You may add theory and interpretation later, but you never want to abandon completely the tears over the stupid father who cannot see the loyalty and love of his abandoned daughter. You never want to let go of that initial emotion.

Sontag was telling me to read books with my body, read with my senses, my heart, my blood, as well as my mind. Read sensuously as well as analytically. Feel the text, grope with it, dream with it, embroider on it: that's what Sontag was telling me. There are limits to analysis, limits to theoretical constructs imposed by the mind on living, shifting pools of literature.

Art begins in magic, Sontag says. With incantation. "In a culture whose already classical dilemma is the hypertrophy of the intellect at the expense of energy and sensual capability, interpretation is the revenge of the intellect upon art ... the revenge of the intellect upon the world." She goes on, "Real art has the capacity to make us nervous. By reducing the work of art to its content and then interpreting that, one tames the work of art. Interpretation makes art manageable, comfortable." Sontag clarifies what she means by interpretation. "Directed to art, interpretation means plucking a set of elements (the X, the Y, the Z, and so forth) from the whole work. The task of interpretation says, Look, don't you see that X is really – or, really means – A? That Y is really B? That Z is really C?" The old style of interpretation, Sontag informs, "... was insistent, but respectful; it erected another meaning on top of the literal one. The modern style of interpretation excavates, and as it excavates, destroys; it digs 'behind' the text, to find a sub-text which is the true one." She sees Marx and Freud as two early practitioners of this modern school of archaeological criticism.

I don't know what Sontag would have made of Said's literary criticism. Her son, David Rieff, refers to Said in *Swimming in a Sea of Death* as "a great friend of hers", but he wasn't a friend she had much to say about. She did admire the way in which Said courageously fought his leukemia: "Said's treatments made his stomach swell up to the size of a pregnant woman in her third trimester. And he suffered indescribable pain. But as my mother repeated over and over again (he had died some months before she was diagnosed with MDS), 'look at all the work he got done with those extra years.'" Work was a holy word in the Sontag lexicon. As for Said on Sontag, he preferred early Sontag to late Sontag, presumably *Against Interpretation* to her novels and later works of criticism.

The two polymaths approach text quite differently. Said shines his own inimitable light on the artistic diamond, but not before looking at the mines, the miners, the politics and big-power greed that went into its making. The social surround is always an essential part of the work of art itself. His strength as a critic is to honour the work – the diamond – while at the same time doing nothing to minimize the significance of the power relations that made production possible. If Said had lived long enough for another major work of critical thought, it might have been entitled, *The Work, the Workers and the Working Environment*. The word, in Said, is always entwined with the world; it always has something to do with work.

Sontag raises her voice in defence of the inviolability of an artwork, and the need for the reader, or viewer, to feel it, hear it, see it, even to be shattered by it, in its wholeness, its dangerousness, its shock, without translation into theoretical constructs and restrictive boxes. I think I was about 19 when I first read Sontag. I was later to add Gaston Bachelard, John Berger, Hélène Cixous, Carole Maso and even Marin Heidegger to my repertoire of how to enter a text. But Sontag was the first to move me from interpretation to celebration, from analysis to embroidery. I first applied Sontag's principles to my essay in *Brick* (Number 44, Summer 1992) on Cavafy's "Ithaca". (Cavafy somehow erroneously – and embarrassingly – got printed as "Cafavy".) In the essay, I tried to connect rather than dissect, stitch rather than unravel. I drew from textile metaphors over those associated with war, archaeology or medicine.

My first encounter with Edward Said came through his book *The World, the Text and the Critic,* and a particular essay in the book, "Swift as Intellectual", quite simply the best essay that I had ever read on the warrior-pamphleteer and polemicist Jonathan Swift.

Said characterizes Swift as a local writer, a reactive writer, someone who responds to some local wrong with correctional intent through satire, irony and parody. Said constructs three theses around Swift: 1. "Swift has no reserve capital: his writing brings to the surface all he has to say … what is being said is being said at that moment, for that moment, by a creature of that moment." 2. "Swift is invariably attacking what he impersonates … to become the thing he attacks, which is … a style or a manner of discourse." 3. "Ahead of his critics, Swift is always aware … that what he is doing above all is *writing* in a world of power." In sum, Said sees Swift as engaged in a writerly project to oppose "human aggression or organized human violence". In this grand project, Swift "was able to place such disparate things as war itself … conquest, colonial oppression, religious factionalism, the manipulations of minds and bodies, schemes for projecting power on nature, on human beings, and on history, the tyranny of the majority, monetary profit for its own sake, the victimization of the poor by a privileged oligarchy." The writer as warrior. Swift is a warrior-writer, and so is Said.

Said's summary of Swift carries into a short masterwork, *Representations of the Intellectual,* where Said spells out specific qualities of the intellectual. He or she must not be beholden to a power centre: the corporation, the government or the university;

must as far as possible avoid slavish specialization; must be an amateur, in its root sense of being a lover, a lover of truth, even if it collides with sacred or official texts. In words with which I think Susan Sontag would concur, the intellectual must be "a thinking and concerned member of a society ... entitled to raise moral issues at the heart of even the most technical and professionalized activity ..."

The intellectual must "question patriotic nationalism, corporate thinking, and a sense of class, racial or gender privilege". This role cannot be played without raising "embarrassing questions or confronting orthodoxy and dogma ..." The intellectual is "someone who cannot easily be co-opted by governments or corporations ..." He or she belongs on the same side with the weak and unrepresented. The intellectual is always "a traveler, a provisional guest, not a freeloader, conqueror, or raider". According to Said, "The intellectual in exile is necessarily ironic, skeptical, even playful – but not cynical." (One wonders if he is again thinking of Swift here.) "Exile means that you are always going to be marginal, and that what you do as an intellectual has to be made up because you cannot follow a prescribed path."

These words about the qualifications necessary to assert one's status as an intellectual apply as much to Sontag as to Said, although Sontag is much more the dilettante and dabbler in world politics. The closest she comes to Said's lifelong disciplined commitment to Palestine is her brief, but nevertheless brave, commitment to a Balkan city under siege.

Where Said applies his theory of the intellectual directly into practice lies in his championing of Palestine against Israeli military might, the US press, popular belief and the possibility of generous remuneration for keeping quiet. As Swift picked up the pen for Ireland with no possibility of financial or governmental reward, so Said picks up the pen for Palestine and has his Columbia University office blown up. Said is undeterred. He continues to give voice to the voiceless. In one of his final talks, "The Public Role of Writers and Intellectuals", published in *Humanism and Democratic Criticism,* he returns to a central concern: the intellectual and Palestine. While dismissing liberals such as Michael Ignatieff who "urge more destruction and death for distant civilians under the banner of benign imperialism", he advocates for a position where: "The intellectual is perhaps a kind of counter-memory, with its own counterdiscourse that will not allow conscience to look away or fall asleep."

He arrives at a point of view on Palestine and Israel similar to Sontag's 1973 documentary film *Promised Lands* in which the conflict was "not a struggle between truth and falsehood but between two opposing, partial truths". Similarly Said can say, "No matter how I have searched for a resolution to this impasse, I cannot find one, for this is not a facile case of right versus right. It cannot be right ever to deprive an entire people of their land and heritage." It is not just to ask a people to live with checkpoints and divided enclaves on less than 20% of their original land; neither is it just to ask Israelis who have occupied the land for a generation to return to Europe. Said concludes: "The Jews too are what I have called a community of suffering and have brought with them a heritage of great tragedy." The Jews and the Palestinians have "Overlapping yet irreconcilable experiences ..."

In The Oscar Romero Award Keynote Address entitled "On Courage and Resistance" and published in *At the Same Time,* Sontag recognizes the wounds of both societies and the need to move beyond them:

> *A wounded and fearful country, Israel, is going through the greatest crisis of its turbulent history, brought about by the*

policy of steadily increasing and reinforcing settlements on the territories won after its victory in the Arab-Israeli war of 1967. The decision of successive Israeli governments to retain control over the West Bank and Gaza, thereby denying their Palestinian neighbors a state of their own, is a catastrophe – moral, human, and political – for both peoples. The Palestinians need a sovereign state. Israel needs a sovereign Palestinian state …

She goes on to thank "courageous Israeli Jewish witnesses, journalists, architects, poets, novelists, professors – among others – who have described and documented and protested and militated against the sufferings of the Palestinians living under the increasingly cruel terms of Israeli military subjugation and settler annexation".

Said was aware of courageous Israelis but seldom spoke of them. He did, however, in a conversation with the Jewish feminist scholar Jacqueline Rose remember vividly a particular Jewish woman. At a forum organized by the Jewish magazine *Tikkun* he found himself reprimanded by the Jewish-American philosopher Michael Waltzer for speaking of the Palestinian and Israeli past. He was told to stop speaking of the past.

The audience was, I would say, about 99 percent Jewish. When he said it, my mouth hung open, but I didn't say anything, because a woman in the audience – I'll never forget this as long as I live, her name was Hilda Silverstein – got up and started – well, it would be too strong to say she started screaming – but she started vociferously attacking Waltzer. She said: "How dare you say that to a Palestinian. How dare you say that to anybody. Because of all the people in the world, we ask the world to remember our past. And you're telling a Palestinian to forget the past? How dare you?" It was an extraordinary thing. And he didn't utter a word after that.

In an interview with the Israeli *Ha'aretz Magazine,* in Tel Aviv, 2000, Said's interviewer, Ari Shavit, comments that Said sounds "very Jewish". Said sportingly replies: "Of course. I'm the last Jewish intellectual ... The only true follower of Adorno. Let me put it this way: I'm a Jewish-Palestinian." In the last few years of his life, Said worked on his "Jewish" works: the posthumously published *Freud and the Non-European* (2003); *Humanism and Democratic Criticism* (2004), which includes a tribute to Erich Auerbach's *Mimesis;* and *On Late Style: Music and Literature Against the Grain* (2006) with an important chapter on Theodor Adorno.

A Jewish-Palestinian. An elegant stylist in clothes and language. The man with unbearably sad eyes. The man whom Nadine Gordimer characterizes as principally a man of music in his dream life – I would also say a man of letters – if he'd been able to resist the call to solidarity and protest from fellow Palestinians. He may reach future generations not as a musician nor a musical theorist nor literary critic but as an eloquent spokesman for those who suffer from injustice. Maybe it is perversely fitting that for some – as with *The New York Times* initially – Said is the intellectual with a stone in his hand; the intellectual who throws it at a tank. It's not enough to dream the world or write it; one has to try to act in it. At the very least, one of his sentences ought to come forward into the world's future: "... the Other is always one of us, not a remote alien."

Closing Time

JOHN BERGER WOULD EMBRACE Edward Said's words on human solidarity, on how the other is always us. Likewise, it's not difficult to picture him framing the words of Muriel Rukeyser in "Waterlily Fire":

> Whatever can come to a city can come to this city …
> Whatever can happen to a woman can happen to me …
> Whatever can happen to anyone can happen to me …

Of the writers I've discussed in this book, the one that lingers for me is John Berger – someone interested in art, storytelling and justice is irresistible to me. The lives of the self-critical Weil and the engaged Said also speak to me but perhaps not as deeply. Like Edward Said, "I came to be terribly interested in the work of John Berger, *Another Way of Telling,* in that whole defense against these master narratives." Berger has a knack of giving everyone – stagehands, one-line actors, understudies, fill-ins, the unrecognized and the forgotten – a voice on the human stage.

Harold Bloom's writing on religion and the strangeness of literature interests me, Susan Sontag's essays, "Against

Interpretation" and "On Style" in particular, still hold up for me, Muriel Rukeyser's poem "Haying Before Storm" I still return to, Robert Lax's *21 Pages* and Leonard Cohen's "Magic is Afoot" continue to give me shivers, but it's John Berger's meditative art in words that chimes with my own preoccupations and dreams.

Berger's personal story resonates for me. So little formal education and yet so well educated! When once asked about his limited formal education, he replied:

> *I would say I had two educations, one from the age of about 16 to 30, when I found myself in London. The company I kept was largely European refugees from fascism – political, mostly Jewish refugees. They were all somewhat older than I and were, I won't say unwelcome, but not very prosperous.*
>
> *They were painters, writers, philosophers, historians. From these people I learned about history in a continental sense, and about politics in a sense much wider than that of the public debates going on then in England.*
>
> *My second education came much later. It began about 25 years ago, when I moved to a village in the Alps. The people there, with whom I became quite close, were older peasants who had once been the children of subsistence farmers. From them I learned a lot about nature, the land, the seasons and a set of priorities by which they tried to live. I learned quite a lot of practical, physical tasks and a kind of ethical code.*

Berger's tribute to unnamed refugees and peasants brings to life a statement of his that I've already quoted: "The number of lives that enter any one life is incalculable."

Berger's style attracts me. I define style as Sontag did in her essay "On Style" as "the signature of the artist's will". According to Sontag, "Every style is a means of insisting on something." Berger's signature, what he insists on, is art, verbal and pictorial, that allows room for history, biography and politics, that has as its base or its end a concern for justice. Style in Berger is a complete presentation of a self on paper, a self connected to others, to community. Berger in every book, in every story or essay, lives the words that Leonard Cohen uses to open his concerts: "I don't have much to give you, but I'm going to give you everything I've got." He recognizes, with Sontag, that: "Writing is finally a series of permissions you give yourself to be expressive in certain ways. To leap. To fly. To fail." He has failed in some works, but he has also leapt and flown in many others.

His sensitivity to the natural world and fellow creatures stands out for me. Who but Berger can read Homer's *The Iliad* and make a point of noticing that the epic poem speaks of a horse's death in the same grave tones that it speaks of a soldier's death? Who but Berger can remark on the relationship between a farmer and a pig that the farmer loves his pig and eats him? The "and" is key here. Berger doesn't use "but" to qualify or diminish the force of the love; he conjoins love and savagery as if they are part of a single action. To live on a farm, to keep pigs and to rely on their meat, is simultaneously to love the animal and to recognize the need to kill it.

Berger looks unsentimentally at the web of life and the human strand within it. In that most lyrical of books, *And Our Faces, My Heart, Brief as Photos,* he finds a seamless way to stitch poetry to prose, art to language, animals to humans, critique to celebration, and life to death. He is a master of the telling detail such as this one about cats: "Cats display more pleasure when licking one another than when eating." The reason is that the urgency of eating displaces pleasure and pleasure only "comes as a plenitude after the act of eating".

A few days ago, I picked up Berger's short story called "A Brush" in *Harper*'s (August 2010). It's a story about reticence, manners, conversation, gift-giving and art. It's also a story about Cambodia, Pol Pot, the Khmer Rouge and homelessness. The narrator begins, "I want to tell you the story of how I gave away this Sho Japanese brush." There is a drawing of the brush on the first page of the story. I assume that's it's by Berger's hand.

The rest of the story goes like this: The narrator who swims at a municipal Parisian pool in the suburbs notices, and eventually speaks to, a Cambodian woman who swims for about an hour and is helped out of the water by a Southeast Asian man. The three exchange words and the narrator learns that the woman is "distantly related to the family of the famous Prince Sihanouk". She had studied art in Phnom Penh, and fled to Europe in the mid-seventies during the reign of terror of Pol Pot and the Khmer Rouge. "Do you still paint?" the narrator asks. "She lifted her left hand into the air, making a gesture of releasing a bird ..."

The woman suffers from "polyarthritis". When she's in the water she weighs less and her joints stop hurting.

The narrator gives the Cambodian woman his Sho brush. Time passes. When next she sees the narrator, she kisses him twice on both cheeks. She, some time later, gives him a painting of a bird, a blue tit, on a bamboo shoot. "The bamboo is drawn according to all the rules of the art." At the end of the story – it's only four magazine pages – the narrator is leafing through a Larousse illustrated encyclopedia and comes upon a blue tit perched at the same angle as the tit in his painting.

The last line of the story is: "And again I understood a little more about homelessness."

Berger's ethics seems to intrude upon his aesthetics. Into the narrative the speaker injects a brief history lesson on Cambodia – how the country had been bombarded by US B-52s before the Khmer Rouge seized power, how the Khmer Rouge "transformed themselves into fanatics so that they could inflict vengeance on reality itself, so they could reduce reality to a single dimension", how today Cambodia is a sweatshop nation with 75 per cent of its exports brand-name merchandise for the multinationals of the West. He even insists on communicating certain details on the geography of Cambodia – that in Khmer, Teuk-Dey means Water-Land, that its flat alluvial plain "is crossed by six major rivers including the vast Mekong". "During and after the summer monsoon rains, the flow of this river multiplies by fifty!"

The speaker assumes a teacherly role with the reader. Do the mini-talks on Cambodia enhance or detract from the story? The story at heart has to do with art and intimacy. How the love of art brings two strangers together in a degree of intimacy in what would otherwise be a fleeting, and unremarkable, encounter in a swimming pool. Is there room for history, geography and politics in such a short tale? Berger makes room. His is the art of inclusion.

You can imagine Hemingway writing this story – Hemingway of *In Our Time,* say, and to be even more specific, Hemingway of "Cat in the Rain". Do you remember the story? A woman in a hotel room looks out the window to a cat seeking shelter from the rain. The woman edges closer and closer to hysteria as she more and more identifies with the cat in its vulnerability, while her husband continues to read. She wants the cat, she wants to protect it, wants to rescue it.

"A Brush" in Hemingway's hands would consist of a man and woman meeting at a pool, connecting for some unnamed reason, and inexplicably exchanging gifts. If Berger needed four pages for the story, Hemingway could do it in two. And instead of periodic injections of history and politics there would be more literary tension and indeterminacy. Hemingway's style is the art of exclusion, of evasion and suggestiveness. Literature in early Hemingway is a pure thing untainted by politics or history.

Literature for Berger is small l. It's a part of – rather than apart from – other modes of human expression; it's a hybrid that is enriched by cross-pollination from a range of fields and disciplines. How unlike Harold Bloom John Berger is. For Bloom, literature is written with a capital L. Its purity doesn't allow for the intermeshing of political issues or concerns for justice. Bloom is interested in the production of masterpieces, in their hierarchy and ranking. Berger is interested in something quieter and more fragile. Bloom places works of art on particular levels – this is above that – while Berger works from the premise that a hand-carved bird, whatever its technical shortcomings, comes from the same earth and reaches for the same sky as a fully accomplished bronze bird in Brancusi's vast sculptural repertoire.

The speaker in "A Brush" refers to the main character, a Cambodian female artist of some reputation, as L – as if writing her name in full would run the risk of invading her privacy. It would be presumptuous of him to say anything more about her than he says. To what extent, then, is the story a factual encounter, with documentary accuracy as central to the narrative as imaginative leaps of fiction? We don't know. We readers live in the mystery.

Berger's story ends quietly, with reticence, in mystery. There is always more not-told than told in any good telling. There are always what Alberto Manguel calls "missing pages" in any piece of writing, in any book, but, in Berger's words, "A likeness, once caught, carries the mystery of a Being."

Memorable Quotes

John Berger

"Style? A certain lightness. A sense of shame excluding certain actions or reactions. A certain proposition of elegance. The supposition that, despite everything, a melody can be looked for and sometimes found."

"The number of lives that enter any one life is incalculable."

"All you have to know is whether you're lying or whether you're trying to tell the truth …"

Harold Bloom

"One mark of originality that can win canonical status for a literary work is a strangeness that we either never altogether assimilate, or that becomes such a given that we are blinded to its idiosyncrasies."

"We read deeply for varied reasons, most of them familiar: that we cannot know enough people profoundly enough; that we need to know ourselves better; that we require knowledge, not just of self and others, but of the way things are."

"What is supposed to be the very essence of Judaism – which is the notion that it is by study that you make yourself a holy people – is nowhere present in Hebrew tradition before the end of the first or the beginning of the second century of the Common Era. It is perfectly clear that the notion reached the Rabbis directly or indirectly from the writings of Plato, because it is a thoroughly Platonic notion. And yet it has become more characteristic of normative Jewish tradition than of any other Western tradition still available to us. I take that to be an instance of why one should distrust any statements about the ontological or historical purity or priority of any spiritual tradition whatsoever."

"Reading, teaching, and writing are for me three words for the one act of the mind."

Leonard Cohen

"I don't have much to give you, but I'm going to give you everything I've got." (Spoken words at a Cohen concert.)

"It is strange that even now prayer is my natural language."

"O God, show me that the Ceremony belongs to Thee. Reveal to your servant a fissure in the Ritual. Change Thy World with the jawbone of a broken Idea. O my Lord, play with me."

"What is a saint? A saint is someone who has achieved a remote human possibility. It is impossible to say what that possibility is. I think it has something to do with the energy of love."

Robert Lax

*be
gin
by
be
ing
pa
tient*

*what bliss
to
be
one
of
the
be
ings*

*the face of one
waiting & waiting*

waiting & waiting

*waiting for a
good he knows
he cannot
make*

Alberto Manguel

"When the library lamps are lit, the outside world disappears and nothing but this space of books remains in existence."

"On the Web, where all texts are equal and alike in form, they become nothing but phantom text and photographic image."

"For Borges, the core of reality lay in books; reading books, writing books, talking about books."

"No literary text is utterly original, no literary text is completely unique, … it stems from previous texts, built on quotations and misquotations, on the vocabularies fashioned by others and transformed through imagination and use."

Muriel Rukeyser

> *To be a Jew in the twentieth century*
> *Is to be offered a gift. If you refuse,*
> *Wishing to be invisible, you choose*
> *Death of the spirit, the stone insanity*
> *Accepting, take full life. Full agonies: …*

"There is also, in any history, the buried, the wasted, and the lost."

The potflower on the windowsill says to me
In words that are green-edged red leaves:
Flower flower flower flower
Today for the sake of all the dead. Burst into flower.

Whatever can come to a city can come to this city ...
Whatever can happen to a woman can happen to me ...
Whatever can happen to anyone can happen to me ...

Edward Said

"For me, sleep is death, as is any diminishment in awareness ... Sleeplessness for me is a cherished state, to be desired at almost any cost; there is nothing for me as invigorating as the early-morning shedding of the shadowy half-consciousness of a night's loss, reacquainting myself with what I might have lost completely a few hours earlier. I occasionally experience myself as a cluster of flowing currents. I prefer this to the idea of a solid self ... These currents, like the themes of one's life, are borne along during the waking hours, and at their best require no reconciling, no harmonizing."

"The intellectual is perhaps a kind of countermemory, with its own counterdiscourse that will not allow conscience to look away or fall asleep."

"... the Other is always one of us, not a remote alien."

Susan Sontag

"If literature has engaged me as a project, first as a reader and then as a writer, it is as an extension of my sympathies to other selves, other domains, other dreams, other words, other territories of concern."

"A writer is first of all a reader. It is from reading that I derive the standards by which I measure my own work and according to which I fall lamentably short. It is from reading, even before writing, that I became part of a community – the community of literature – which includes more dead than living writers."

"Love words, agonize over sentences. And pay attention to the world."

"In a culture whose already classical dilemma is the hypertrophy of the intellect at the expense of energy and sensual capability, interpretation is the revenge of the intellect upon art ... the revenge of the intellect upon the world. Real art has the capacity to make us nervous. By reducing the work of art to its content and then interpreting that, one tames the work of art. Interpretation makes art manageable, comfortable."

"All my work says be serious, be passionate, wake up."

"If books disappear, history will also disappear, and human beings will also disappear ... Books are not only the arbitrary sum of our dreams, and our memory. They also give us the model of self-transcendence."

"Literature is the house of nuance and contrariness against the voice of simplification."

Simone Weil

"Every human being cries out silently to be read differently."

"No poetry concerning the people is authentic if fatigue does not figure in it, and the hunger and thirst which come from fatigue."

"Justice consists in seeing that no harm is done to men. Whenever a man cries inwardly: 'Why am I being hurt?' harm is being done to him. He is often mistaken when he tries to define the harm, and why and by whom it is being inflicted on him. But the cry itself is infallible."

"Nearly all the *Iliad* takes place far from warm baths. Nearly all human life, then and now, takes place far from hot baths."

Where do books come from?

I believe, as Northrop Frye did, that books come from other books. This one comes from my readings in poetry, biography, theology and literary criticism. It builds on the foundation of a previous book – *Spirit Book Word: An Inquiry into Literature and Spirituality*.

Books also come from conversations. This book comes from conversations with David Cohen, Di Brandt, Marilyn Gear Pilling, Frances Ward, Mark Garber, Wayne Allan, Eric Mader, Susan McCaslin, Michael Higgins, B.W. Powe, Ted Rettig, Dale Behnke, Lee Easton, Bronwyn Drainie, Paul Lisson, Anne McPherson and Jamie Mallory.

Books are sustained by love. This book has been sustained by my wife Cheryl, son Daniel, daughter Rachel, sister Caroline, my grandson Kaizen and my mother and father.

Books also require the faith of a good publisher. I thank Maureen Whyte for her faith in me and this book. Books benefit from the skill and experience of a good editor. I thank George Down for his careful editing of the text. Whatever errors remain are my own.

Acknowledgements

EARLIER VERSIONS OF MY WORK on Leonard Cohen and Alberto Manguel appeared in the *Literary Review of Canada* edited by Bronwyn Drainie. *Hamilton Arts and Letters* edited by Paul Lisson published my thoughts on Muriel Rukeyser and *The Merton Journal: Journal of the Thomas Merton Society of Great Britain and Ireland,* edited by Fiona Gardner and Keith Griffin, first published my response to Robert Lax.